THE WHOLE HUMAN LEADER

PETER SORGENFREI

THE WHOLE HUMAN LEADER

HOW TO LEAD WITHOUT LOSING YOURSELF

WILEY

Published by John Wiley & Sons, Inc., Hoboken, New Jersey.

For general information on our other products and services or for technical support, please contact our Customer Care Department within the United States at (800) 762-2974, outside the United States at (317) 572-3993 or fax (317) 572-4002.

Wiley also publishes its books in a variety of electronic formats. Some content that appears in print may not be available in electronic formats. For more information about Wiley products, visit our website at www.wiley.com.

Library of Congress Cataloging-in-Publication Data:

Names: Sorgenfrei, Peter, author.
Title: The whole human leader : how to lead without losing yourself / Peter Sorgenfrei.
Description: Hoboken, New Jersey : Wiley, [2026] | Includes index.
Identifiers: LCCN 2026010092 (print) | LCCN 2026010093 (ebook) | ISBN 9781394403196 (hardback) | ISBN 9781394403219 (adobe pdf) | ISBN 9781394403202 (epub)
Subjects: LCSH: Leadership.
Classification: LCC HD57.7 .S6927 2026 (print) | LCC HD57.7 (ebook)
LC record available at https://lccn.loc.gov/2026010092
LC ebook record available at https://lccn.loc.gov/2026010093

Cover Design: Wiley
Author Photo: Courtesy of the Author

Printed and bound by CPI Group (UK) Ltd, Croydon, CR0 4YY
C9781394403196_220626

For my parents, who gave me enough when it wasn't easy.

For Joanna, who helps me remember who I am.

For Theo, who shows me every day what matters.

Contents

"The privilege of a lifetime is to become who you truly are."

—Carl Jung

Introduction

The sound of my son's voice carries across the apartment this Sunday morning in Nordhavn, animated conversation with friends online as they build something together in a game I don't fully understand. I'm at my desk with coffee going cold, watching the harbor through the window, and I find myself thinking about all the versions of myself who sat at desks like this one over the past twenty years. The consultant in New York. The strategist in London. The CEO in Copenhagen. Each one was certain he was building something that mattered. Each one was slowly drowning without knowing it.

I founded my first company in 2005, a consulting business born of my restlessness with corporate life. I'd spent years at Toyota, where I became the youngest manager in company history, and then at UBS on Wall Street, where I learned that being good at analyzing companies didn't mean I wanted to spend my life doing it. The consulting business was supposed to be different. It was supposed to give me freedom.

That first company led to five more over the next two decades, across three countries. I built teams, raised capital, navigated failures, and celebrated successes. The last company before my breakdown was Holo, which became Europe's largest autonomous vehicle operator. Seventy employees across five countries. Technology that didn't exist when we started. A vision of the future we were making real.

From the outside, I had built exactly the career I'd imagined. From the inside, I was coming apart. My marriage was eroding. My body was keeping score of every boundary I ignored. I was performing the exhausting theater of having it all figured out while something essential was slowly dying.

Then one morning, I simply couldn't move. My body had made the decision my mind refused to make. I lay in bed, unable to get up, my brain and body no longer connected. The psychologist would later explain it as the neural pathways becoming so overloaded that they had essentially shut down. For days, my sister cared for me while I existed in a fog, an empty shell with things happening around me that I couldn't quite register. I wasn't making decisions. I wasn't fighting back. I was just there, disconnected from the life I had spent two decades building.

Listening now to my son coordinate with his friends, I recognize something I couldn't see back then: This moment is what integration looks like. Not balance, not compromise, not having it all. Integration. The practice of refusing to fragment yourself into versions that look impressive while abandoning the sustainable one.

This is a book about that integration. About moving from the exhausting performance of leadership to the sustainable practice of leading as a whole human being.

The Crisis You're Not Supposed to Talk About

Nobody tells you about this part of success: the higher you climb, the more fragmented you become. You learn to compartmentalize brilliantly. The leader who has all the answers. The partner who's physically present but emotionally absent. The parent who's always working. The friend who's too busy to show up. The human who's forgotten how to be simple.

We're taught to call this "professionalism." We're rewarded for it with promotions, recognition, and the persistent myth that sustainable success is just one more optimization away.

But I've worked with enough leaders across enough cultures to know the truth: We're not optimizing our way to wholeness. We're fragmenting our way to crisis.

Since my own breakdown in 2020, I've coached founders and CEOs across thirteen countries, working with more than forty senior leaders each year. I've sat across from CEOs in Berlin who can't sleep without pharmaceutical assistance. COOs in Stockholm are managing billion-dollar operations while their marriages dissolve. Managing directors in London are making decisions that affect thousands, yet barely manage their own well-being. Founders in San Francisco are building the future while burning out their teams and themselves.

The pattern is universal, even when its expression varies by culture. In some places, we call it ambition. In others, dedication. In Denmark, where I grew up, we have a word, *nok*, that means "enough." It's a word that suggests sufficiency, completion, a sense that what you have is what you need. It's a word that high-achieving leaders have largely lost the ability to use about themselves.

What's Changed Since I Started This Work

When I started coaching leaders after my own recovery, the conversations happened behind closed doors. Leaders would admit their struggles only in the safety of a confidential session, terrified that their boards or teams would discover their humanity.

Something has shifted. The COVID-19 pandemic accelerated a reckoning that was already underway. Remote work erased the boundaries between professional and personal, making fragmentation impossible to sustain. Artificial intelligence is now accelerating the pace of change, intensifying the pressure while promising to help us manage it. Leaders are burning out faster, even as the tools meant to support them multiply.

The executives I work with today are more willing to name what's happening. They're asking different questions. Not "How do I perform at a higher level?" but "How do I sustain this?" Not "How do I project confidence?" but "How do I lead authentically?" Not "How do I have it all?" but "How do I have what matters?"

This book is my attempt to answer those questions. Not with abstract theory, but with the hard-won wisdom of someone who crashed, lost nearly everything, rebuilt, and now helps others do the same.

How to Use This Book

The book follows a four-act structure that mirrors the journey from fragmentation to integration.

- Act 1 (Chapters 1–3) explores the breaking point. We'll look at why success doesn't equal security, how high performers learn to suffer in silence, and what it looks like when the system you've built starts to crack. If you're picking up this book because something feels unsustainable, these chapters will help you understand what's happening and why.
- Act 2 (Chapters 4–7) digs into the reckoning. We'll examine energy as the real currency of leadership, what happens to relationships when work consumes everything, how to move from solo heroics to distributed leadership, and the systematic approach to recovery when you've pushed too far. This is the messy middle, the place where old patterns are dismantled, and new ones begin to form.
- Act 3 (Chapters 8–10) introduces the Whole Human Framework, an integrated approach to leadership that enables sustainable success. We'll explore what it means to shift from hero to human, and how to have the difficult conversations that integration requires.
- Act 4 (Chapters 11–12) focuses on integration in practice. What do your people need from you? How do you design a life you don't want to escape from? These chapters turn insight into action.

Each chapter opens with a scene. These aren't dramatizations or composite characters. They're real moments from my work with leaders across cultures, rendered with the kind of sensory detail that I hope will make abstract concepts feel immediate and visceral. I've changed names and identifying details to protect confidentiality, but the struggles are real.

You'll notice the voice shifts throughout. Sometimes I speak directly to you. Sometimes I share my own story. Sometimes I step back to observe patterns across the leaders I've worked with. This isn't an inconsistency. It's integration itself, the willingness to show up in different ways depending on what the moment requires.

At the end of each chapter, you'll find reflection questions and practical tools. Use them or don't. Some readers will want to work through every exercise. Others will discover value simply in the recognition that their experience is shared. Both approaches are valid.

One suggestion: Resist the temptation to read this book the way you read everything else, quickly, efficiently, extracting the key points and moving on. The practice of integration requires a different kind of attention. Slow down. Let the stories live with you. Notice what resonates and what triggers resistance. The discomfort might be pointing toward something meaningful.

The Invitation

My son's voice has shifted from laughter to a focused collaboration, the tone teenagers use when they're problem-solving with friends on voice chat and building something together, iterating, trying different approaches. There's something in that pattern worth paying attention to: build, test, adjust, try again differently.

That's what integration looks like. Not a destination you arrive at once and then maintain forever, but an ongoing practice of building, testing, adjusting, trying again. Some days you'll get it right. Some days you'll fall back into old patterns. The point isn't perfection. The fact is, the continued willingness to try again differently.

I don't know where you are in your journey. You may be at the edge of crisis, recognizing the signs I'll describe in the early chapters. Perhaps you've already crashed, and you're looking for a way to rebuild. You may be curious about whether there's a better way to lead and live.

Wherever you are, this book is an invitation. Not to become someone different, but to become more fully yourself. Not to optimize your way to a better life, but to integrate the pieces that achievement culture has fragmented.

From the harbor, I can hear the sound of weekend sailors preparing their boats, the clatter and conversation of people doing something they choose to do, not something they have to do. That's the quality this book is after. Not the elimination of work or ambition, just the integration of it with everything else that makes life worth living.

Come. Let's begin.

1 Success Is Not Security

Why achievement doesn't protect you from collapse, and how to spot early signs of misalignment.

The sunlight streams through the windows of Soho House Copenhagen, casting long shadows across the leather chairs and wooden coffee tables. It's 4:47 p.m. on a Tuesday in August, and the usual creative buzz of the club feels subdued in the golden hour. I'm waiting for Henrik, a CEO whose company I've been asked to help navigate through what his board diplomatically calls "organizational challenges."

In reality, Henrik is exhausting his entire leadership team. He's accomplished everything the business world admires. However, his HR director called me because three senior executives have resigned in the past few months, all citing "unsustainable demands" and "impossible expectations."

A waiter approaches our corner table, balancing a coffee service on his tray. He pauses, scanning the room uncertainly before asking a nearby member if the order is for her. The slight confusion feels fitting—even in spaces designed for comfort and connection, we sometimes lose our way.

In the quiet before Henrik arrives, I am not the leadership coach with systematic approaches to personal transformation, not the former founder who built something meaningful from nothing, and not the consultant who has worked with leaders from Tokyo to Toronto. I am just a fifty-one-year-old man who knows what it feels like to be extraordinarily capable and completely depleted at the same time.

Henrik's footsteps echo on the polished herringbone wood floors. Soon, he'll walk through the lounge carrying the same burden I once bore—the exhausting weight of believing that his worth as a person depends on his performance as a leader. We'll spend the next hour discussing organizational design and team dynamics. But really, we'll be talking about something much more fundamental: the difference between success and security and why high achievers often confuse the two.

The Breakdown That Changed Everything

My own realization didn't come suddenly, no heart attack or collapse in a boardroom, just a Monday morning in February 2020 when I couldn't get out of bed. My brain and body had disconnected, like a computer running too many programs for too long and finally crashing.

The automotive technology startup I helped found in 2016 gave me the feeling that exceptional efforts and achievements could build lasting security. We were developing autonomous vehicle systems—advanced technology, significant funding, a talented team, and a clear(ish) market opportunity. Each funding allocation felt like validation. Every customer project confirmed we were on the right path. Industry recognition and media coverage indicated we were creating something meaningful for society.

But during those same three years of external success, something else was happening—something I was too busy achieving to notice. The relentless pace needed to keep momentum was slowly draining my ability for everything else. Relationships took a back seat to business development. Health became something to optimize rather than nurture. Rest became, well, restless.

The stress of maintaining constant growth while navigating uncharted regulatory terrain was relentless. The pressure to project confidence while dealing with daily technical setbacks was exhausting. The responsibility for seventy people's livelihoods while operating in an industry that barely existed felt overwhelming.

During the ensuing twelve weeks away from work on sick leave, the board made a decision that felt both unavoidable and surprising: They let me go. Not because I was incapable or because the company was struggling, but because they needed leadership that could handle the specific pressures of our situation. It was, they assured me, nothing personal—just business.

But it felt deeply personal because I had built my entire sense of security around being "the CEO who built something amazing from nothing." When that identity was taken away, I realized I had no real foundation beneath it.

During those twelve weeks of forced stillness, I discovered something that contradicted everything I believed about professional success: Achievement and security are not the same. In fact, when pursued the wrong way, extraordinary achievement can make you more fragile instead of more resilient.

Two Definitions of Worth

This realization forced me to review the conflicting messages about success and security that influenced my leadership approach.

My Danish family valued *tryghed*, a deep sense of security that stems from community, authenticity, and sustainable rhythms. *Tryghed* isn't built through individual achievement; it's nurtured through belonging, through contributing to something larger than oneself, through knowing that your worth isn't based on your performance.

But the American context in which I was building my early career operated under entirely different rules. Here, security came directly from achievement. The more you accomplished, the safer you became. The higher you climbed, the more protected you were from life's uncertainties. Success wasn't just rewarding—it was armor against an unpredictable world.

Working on Wall Street at UBS, I noticed something interesting about the most successful people around me. Despite accomplishing great things—running businesses worth hundreds of millions, earning salaries that would make them financially secure for life, and being recognized as leaders in their fields—many still seemed deeply anxious about their futures.

The partners at major firms worked longer hours than junior associates. Senior executives appeared more concerned about performance reviews than those just starting their careers. The most accomplished individuals often looked the most worried about maintaining their positions.

This wasn't a weakness or character flaw—it was the logical outcome of building security through achievement. When your sense of safety relies on continuous performance, you become stuck in a never-ending cycle of proving your worth. Early in your career, failure meant learning and trying again. But once you've built an identity around producing superior results, failure threatens not only your current success but also your entire sense of self.

For fifteen years, I unconsciously followed this American pattern: If I could just accomplish enough, build something impressive enough, and prove my abilities convincingly enough, then I would finally feel secure in the world. Each milestone, first client, first employee, first office, first revenue goal met, felt like another layer of protection against uncertainty.

I was building what I believed was a foundation of security, one achievement at a time. What I was creating was a house of cards that would fall the moment I couldn't sustain the performance that held it together.

That anxiety I observed on Wall Street twenty years ago has only intensified. Today, the leaders I work with face a new dimension of insecurity: The sense that their expertise itself might become obsolete. Artificial intelligence has accelerated the pace at which knowledge becomes commoditized. The analysis that once took senior consultants days now takes junior analysts hours, with AI doing the heavy lifting. The strategic insight that distinguished seasoned executives can increasingly be approximated by systems that never sleep.

I watch leaders respond to this shift in predictable ways. Some double down on achievement, working harder to stay ahead of tools that don't get tired. Others chase the latest AI certification, hoping that mastering the technology will restore their sense of security. A few retreat into denial, insisting their expertise can never be replicated.

What I've learned from working with leaders navigating this shift: AI doesn't change the fundamental equation. It reveals it. If your security was always built on what you know rather than who you are, AI simply accelerates the exposure. If your identity depends on being the smartest person in the room, you're now competing with systems that have read more than any human ever could.

The leaders who find stability in this new landscape aren't the ones who outrun the technology. They're the ones who have already built security on something AI cannot replicate: judgment developed through experience, relationships built on trust, wisdom about what matters and why. They've learned what I learned during those twelve weeks of stillness: that real security was never about achievement in the first place.

The Success-Security Matrix: Four Ways of Being

Currently working as a coach with founders and senior executives across various industries and cultures, I've noticed four distinct patterns in how people relate to achievement and stability. Recognizing these patterns helps us understand where we are and where we want to go. Essentially it is a matrix composed of internal stability on one dimension and external achievement on the other.

High Success + High Security: Sustainable Excellence

These are leaders who have gained significant external recognition while maintaining a strong sense of personal stability and authenticity. They have learned to pursue achievement in ways that support, rather than compromise, their core well-being. Their success feels aligned with their values, relationships, and sense of purpose.

What sets this group apart isn't a lack of ambition, but the foundation they stand on. They work hard because they care about the result, not because they need outside validation to feel worthy. They take risks because they believe in the mission, not because they are running from their fears. Most importantly, their identity stays steady regardless of short-term results.

High Success + Low Security: The Danger Zone

This is where most high-achieving leaders find themselves: externally successful but internally fragile. They've accomplished impressive things, but often at the expense of their health, relationships, or sense of authentic self. Their success feels unstable, requiring constant vigilance to maintain.

This was me in February 2020: outwardly successful, but internally exhausted and disconnected from any real stability or satisfaction. The achievements were genuine, but they fostered dependence rather than freedom, anxiety rather than peace. Every new challenge felt like a threat to a carefully built identity rather than an interesting problem to solve.

Low Success + High Security: Hidden Potential

These individuals might not have gained widespread recognition yet, but they hold something more valuable: a strong sense of who they are, independent of their achievements. They maintain solid relationships, uphold clear values, and follow sustainable routines. When they do find success, it is both meaningful and enduring because it's built on firm foundations.

Low Success + Low Security: The Starting Point

This is where most people begin: without significant external achievement and without internal security. The question becomes: Which should you pursue first? The conventional wisdom suggests chasing success first, then working on security. But what I've learned is that this approach often makes security harder to achieve, not easier.

The Science Behind Achievement and Security

The relationship between external success and internal security is one of the most studied paradoxes in psychology. The research confirms what many high achievers eventually discover: Accomplishment and safety operate on entirely different circuits.

- **The High-Achievement Paradox:** Suniya Luthar's research at Arizona State University followed students in high-achieving schools and found rates of clinically significant anxiety and depression—six to seven times the national average. In 2019, the National Academies of Sciences designated youth in "high-achieving schools" as an official at-risk group, joining poverty and trauma as recognized environmental threats. Achievement-oriented environments don't insulate from distress; they correlate with it.

- **Performance-Contingent Self-Worth:** Jennifer Crocker at the University of Michigan tracked 642 first-year college students and found that students whose self-worth depended on academic performance showed increased self-esteem on acceptance days and decreased self-esteem on rejection days. Their emotional stability was hostage to outcomes. Those basing self-worth on external contingencies were significantly more likely to develop depressive symptoms over time.
- **The Hedonic Treadmill:** Philip Brickman's Northwestern University research compared lottery winners, accident victims, and controls. Eighteen months after winning the lottery, winners were no happier than controls. Subsequent research by Sheldon and Lyubomirsky at UC Riverside confirmed that achievement gains show swift adaptation. We quickly adjust to promotions, requiring further accomplishments to feel the same level of satisfaction.
- **Attachment and Achievement Motivation:** Andrew Elliot and Harry Reis at the University of Rochester documented that insecurely attached adults show higher fear of failure and view achievement settings as threatening. They pursue accomplishment to fill unmet security needs, but external success cannot repair internal working models formed in childhood. Securely attached adults demonstrate approach-based motivation and less fear of failure.

Achievement cannot provide lasting security because it operates on a different psychological system than genuine safety. Success pursued from anxiety produces more anxiety, not less.

What Achievement Can and Cannot Do

Success—real, meaningful achievement—is valuable. It can open doors, provide resources, increase your impact, and give you a sense of purpose. But it cannot guarantee security. In fact, when pursued as the main source of safety, success often weakens what you're truly aiming for.

Security depends on internal stability, while striving for success often leads to internal instability. Security thrives with sustainable patterns, whereas chasing achievement usually requires unsustainable effort. Genuine relationships strengthen security, while results-driven living often views relationships as secondary to performance.

This doesn't mean choosing between success and security—it means understanding that security must come from different sources than achievement. When you have true security, you can pursue success with abundance rather than scarcity, with curiosity rather than desperation, and with service rather than ego.

The leaders who maintain both high performance and deep satisfaction over decades are not necessarily those who achieve the most, but those who succeed in ways that support rather than harm their core well-being.

Throughout my career, I have often heard the phrase "work-life balance" offered as the answer to this dilemma. The belief was that the issue was simply about how time was divided—spending fewer hours working and more on personal life—and that this would naturally ease the anxiety.

But here's what I learned during those twelve weeks of stillness: The problem isn't how you allocate your time. The issue is that when your sense of security depends entirely on professional achievement, no amount of "balance" can bring true peace of mind.

You can cut back your work hours, but if your sense of identity is still linked to your performance, you'll worry about work during your personal time. You can take vacations, but if your self-esteem depends on outside approval, you'll check email while at the beach. You can set boundaries, but if your sense of security is based on achievement, those boundaries will feel like threats to your safety.

Real security comes from a completely different source. It comes from understanding who you are, regardless of your achievements. It is built through forming relationships that aren't just transactional. It is earned by contributing to meaningful causes, whether or not you get recognized.

Leader Spotlight: A Tactical Transformation

Maria runs a sustainable fashion startup in Amsterdam that has grown from three employees to forty-five in two years. When we started working together, she was stuck in a classic high-success, low-security pattern, meeting every growth target while feeling increasingly disconnected from her original mission and her young daughter.

The breakthrough came not from philosophical insight but through specific tactical adjustments. Instead of trying to balance competing priorities, Maria restructured her role to unify them.

First, she started "thinking walks," thirty-minute strolls during which she would address one complex decision each day. "I realized I was making too many decisions in reactive mode," she explains. "The walking gave me space to think systemically instead of just responding to whatever was most urgent."

Second, she shifted from weekly team meetings focused on status updates to bi-weekly strategic sessions where team members brought her decisions to make rather than information to process. "My team was bringing me problems when they were already crises. Now they bring me opportunities when we can still shape the outcome."

Most importantly, she stopped trying to prove her value through availability and began demonstrating it through judgment. "I used to respond to every message within minutes because I thought that showed leadership. But it was training my team to expect instant responses rather than thoughtful ones. When I started taking time to give better answers instead of faster ones, the quality of our decisions improved dramatically."

The result? Maria's company continues to grow quickly, but now she leaves the office at 6:30 p.m. three days a week to have dinner with her daughter. Counterintuitively, her team reports feeling more supported, not less, because the time she does spend with them is more strategic and less reactive.

"The weirdest part is that when I stopped focusing on leadership and just led, work became energizing instead of draining. When I stopped trying to control every result, our outcomes got better."

Cross-Cultural Approaches to Sustainable Achievement

Understanding how diverse cultures view the connection between success and security can help us create more intentional strategies for both.

- **American Approach:** Focuses on individual achievement as the main route to safety and stability. This drives high motivation and strong results but often sacrifices sustainable rhythms and genuine relationships. The strength is ambition; the weakness can be burnout.

- **Scandinavian Approach:** Emphasizes security through community and sustainability, believing that individual success is meaningful only when it benefits the collective well-being. This builds more stable foundations but can sometimes limit ambitious achievement. Its strength is sustainability; a possible weakness is complacency.
- **German Approach:** Values systematic excellence and long-term thinking, building security through competence and reliability rather than dramatic achievement. This creates solid foundations but can sometimes limit creative risk-taking. The strength is thoroughness; the weakness can be rigidity.
- **East Asian Approach:** Often emphasizes family and community security over individual achievement, viewing success as a collective rather than personal accomplishment. This creates strong support systems but can sometimes limit individual expression and innovation. The strength lies in interconnection; the weakness can be conformity.

Understanding these variations helps us create more intentional relationships between achievement and security in our lives and organizations. The most effective leaders I work with borrow elements from different approaches instead of strictly following their cultural default.

What I Wish I'd Known: Security and Success

If I could go back to my younger self, the one who thought that achieving more would automatically lead to feelings of security, I would offer this advice:

- Security isn't something you attain—it's something you nurture. It doesn't arise from gathering external validation but from strengthening internal stability. It's not established through individual achievements but through genuine connections and meaningful contributions.

- Success is most fulfilling when it arises from a sense of security rather than seeking it. When you understand who you are beyond your achievements, you can pursue goals driven by curiosity instead of desperation, by service instead of ego, and by abundance instead of scarcity.
- Most importantly, the question isn't whether to pursue success, but how to succeed in ways that make you more fully human, not less. How to build achievements that feel like expressions of who you are rather than compensation for who you're not.

The Foundation Assessment

Before reading further, take a moment to assess your current relationship between success and security honestly.

Achievement Indicators (Rate 1–5 for each, with 1 for weakest and 5 for strongest indicator):

- External recognition in your field
- Financial compensation relative to peers
- Measurable professional goals met
- Influence and decision-making authority
- Growth trajectory in career or business

Security Indicators (Rate 1–5 for each, with 1 for weakest and 5 for strongest indicator):

- Sense of personal worth independent of results
- Quality of non-transactional relationships
- Ability to be authentic in professional contexts
- Sustainable rhythms that support long-term performance
- Clarity about values and purpose beyond career success

Look at your scores. Where is the gap largest? What would change if you focused on building security first, then pursuing success from that foundation?

Questions for Reflection

Transformational Question: "What would be enough for you?"

This isn't a question of settling for less or lowering your ambitions. It's about recognizing the internal foundation that enables you to pursue external goals with abundance rather than scarcity, driven by curiosity rather than desperation.

Personal Awareness: When have you accomplished something you believed would provide security, only to still feel vulnerable or unsettled?

Systemic Thinking: How does your organization equate achievement with security? Where do you observe this influencing team dynamics or success metrics?

Action-Oriented: What would you do differently this week if you truly believed that success and security are not the same?

Integration: Beyond professional achievements, where else in your life do you chase external validation hoping it will create internal peace? How might building security first change your approach to success in relationships, health, or personal fulfillment?

The Shift from More to Lasting

As I walk home along Copenhagen harbor, where a massive ferry transports people between Denmark and Norway, bridging one way of life and another, I think about Henrik's recognition in his eyes when he left Soho House an hour ago—the same recognition I felt five years ago that something essential needs to change.

The answer isn't about choosing success over security. It's about realizing that true security lays the groundwork for lasting success, while chasing success without security can weaken both. It's about understanding that achievements feel the most fulfilling when they reflect who you are, not when they make up for who you're not.

Success isn't security, but it doesn't have to be risky. The journey toward integration starts with the understanding that we've been asking the wrong question. Not "How can I achieve more?" but "How can I build something that lasts?"

But what happens when high achievers try to build that foundation? When we finally admit we need support, we often discover we've forgotten how to ask for it. In Chapter 2, we'll explore what happens when strength turns into silence, and why the most capable leaders often carry burdens they were never meant to carry alone.

2 The Silence of the Strong

The unseen cost of holding it all together, and how to build systems of real support.

Seven fifteen on a crisp morning along Canary Wharf, and London's financial district is waking up with its own rhythm of determined ambition. The river flows with tidal certainty while above, glass towers catch the early light like massive instruments of precision. I'm walking to meet Priya, a strategy director whose message arrived at midnight a few weeks ago: "I'm dying, not literally, but I need help."

The morning joggers and suited early commuters share the pathway with an unspoken understanding of personal purpose. Each person moves with the kind of determination that defines London: focused, efficient, slightly shielded against the day ahead. But what happens when that personal determination turns into isolation? When strength becomes silence? When does the very competence that earned you a promotion become the barrier preventing others from contributing their best ideas?

Priya arrives promptly at seven thirty, walking with the steady pace of someone who has learned to save energy for the battles that truly matter. We settle into a Pret for a coffee. She orders it black and cuts straight to the point in that direct manner that senior leaders develop when time is their most limited resource.

"I realized last week that I haven't said, 'I don't know' in a professional setting in three years," she begins, stirring her coffee with mechanical precision. "Not once. Even when I genuinely didn't know something, even when admitting uncertainty could have led to better decisions, and even when my team clearly had expertise I lacked. I've been expressing certainty for so long that I've forgotten how to access knowledge, mine or anyone else's."

She pauses, watching a group of office workers cross the street with their morning rush purposefulness.

"The cost of this job isn't just personal exhaustion anymore. It's a disassociation from my colleagues, like I'm a cold robot. They no longer really include me in stuff. They assume I already have answers, that I've figured it out, and expect responses, rather than discussion, when I have no clue."

The Architecture of Professional Silence

What Priya was discovering is one of the most widespread and harmful patterns in modern leadership: turning competence into isolation. The skills that make someone successful as an individual contributor often become obstacles in leadership roles. We perfect the ability to have answers just when our role demands us to become comfortable with questions.

In Denmark, we have a concept called *fællesskab*—roughly translated as "community" or "fellowship," but carrying more profound connotations of shared responsibility and mutual support. True fællesskab requires vulnerability from those in leadership positions. It requires admitting what you don't know, acknowledging what you can't control, and creating space for others to contribute their unique capabilities.

But most leadership development teaches us the opposite. We learn to project confidence, maintain authority, and provide direction even when we're uncertain about the way forward. We're rewarded for having answers, penalized for asking questions, and promoted based on our ability to seem in control of inherently uncertain situations.

The result is a strange kind of professional loneliness that grows stronger as our responsibilities increase. The more senior we become, the less likely we are to show uncertainty, admit our limitations, or ask for help. Just when we need collective intelligence the most, we often isolate ourselves from the very resources that could help us make better decisions.

The Compound Cost of Silence

Currently working with executives across various industries and regions, I've realized that leadership silence incurs compounded costs that go beyond individual stress. When leaders repeatedly pretend to have certainty they do not genuinely feel, it reinforces what systems theorists refer to as "organizational defensive routines," patterns that hinder learning and adaptation.

Consider Sarah, a technology leader on the US East Coast I worked with, whose company was facing challenges due to rapid market shifts. During our first conversation, she described feeling "confident in how our role in the market is evolving" while privately admitting she was overwhelmed by the pace of industry transformation.

"I spend most of my energy managing what I show my team," she explained during a casual coffee (okay, donut and coffee) conversation we had near her office. "If I express uncertainty about strategic direction, they panic. If I admit I'm learning as we go, they lose confidence in leadership. If I acknowledge that some of our assumptions might be wrong, they start hedging instead of executing."

But Sarah's silence was causing exactly the outcomes she wanted to avoid. Her team, sensing her unspoken doubt, started second-guessing decisions in private while carrying them out publicly. They created complex workarounds for things they didn't fully understand. Most importantly, they stopped giving her information she might actually need.

"I realized I was getting promoted for my ability to appear in control," Sarah reflected months later, "but the situations requiring the most control were precisely the ones where appearing in control was least helpful. Market disruption, technology shifts, regulatory changes—these require collective sense-making, not individual certainty."

The breakthrough happened when Sarah started experimenting with what she called "strategic uncertainty," explicitly acknowledging what she didn't know and encouraging her team to consider implications together. Surprisingly, this vulnerability actually boosted her team's confidence in her leadership.

"They started bringing me problems earlier when we could actually solve them," she says now. "They began offering solutions instead of just following orders. Most importantly, they started thinking like owners instead of employees. I realized that my job wasn't to have all the answers, but to create conditions where the best answers could emerge."

The Pressure Pyramid

To understand how professional silence develops and builds over time, I've found it helpful to map what I call the Pressure Pyramid, the organized way that individual responsibility grows as we move up in organizations.

- **Level 1: Personal Impact.** At entry levels, your main responsibility is your own performance. Success involves doing tasks well, meeting deadlines, and supporting team goals. Silence here might mean not asking for help when needed or not admitting when you don't understand expectations.
- **Level 2: Relational Influence.** As you gain experience, your impact extends to direct relationships with colleagues, clients, and stakeholders. Success involves managing these relationships well while maintaining your individual contributions. Silence here often means not addressing interpersonal conflicts or not sharing concerns that might affect team dynamics.
- **Level 3: Strategic Responsibility.** In management roles, your decisions impact multiple people and have longer-term horizons. You're responsible for results you can't directly control, achieved through people you can't micromanage. Silence here usually means not admitting when you lack information needed for good decisions or not recognizing when your strategies aren't working.
- **Level 4: Systemic Leadership.** In senior roles, you're tasked with creating conditions that enable others to succeed, often amid significant uncertainty and complexity. Success depends on orchestrating collective intelligence, not just individual effort. Silence here means failing to foster the collaborative thinking essential for tackling complex challenges.

The dangerous pattern is that skills leading to success at each level often become obstacles at the next. The individual competence that worked at Level 1 turns into a barrier to collaborative leadership at Level 4. The apparent strength that impressed at Level 2 becomes isolation that hampers effectiveness at Level 3.

This pattern has grown more complex in recent years. Artificial intelligence offers what seems like a solution to leadership silence: You can consult AI systems without revealing uncertainty to another human being. Need to think through a strategic decision? Ask AI. Unsure about market dynamics? Let the machine analyze it. Struggling with a difficult conversation? Get coaching from a chatbot.

I've watched leaders embrace these tools to maintain their image of competence while privately seeking the help they need. And on one level, it works. AI can process information, offer frameworks, and help structure thinking. These capabilities are genuinely useful.

What AI cannot do: It cannot provide *fællesskab*. It cannot sit with you in genuine uncertainty and help you feel less alone. It cannot offer the kind of support that comes from another human being who has faced similar challenges and emerged with wisdom to share. It cannot build the relationships of mutual trust that make organizations resilient.

The leaders who use AI as a substitute for human vulnerability often find themselves more isolated, not less. They've added a sophisticated tool to their arsenal while avoiding the fundamental work of building genuine connection. The silence remains. It just becomes more technologically mediated.

What I've observed is that AI makes collective intelligence more important, not less. As routine analysis becomes automated, the distinctly human capacities, judgment, wisdom, relational trust, become the primary source of leadership value. But accessing those capacities requires breaking the silence. It requires admitting what you don't know to people who can help, not just to systems that can process.

The most effective leaders I work with use AI to enhance their thinking while using human relationships to sustain their humanity. They don't confuse having better tools with having better support.

Breaking the Silence: A Systematic Approach

The antidote to professional silence isn't simply "being more vulnerable"—it's developing systematic approaches to sharing appropriate information, uncertainty, and decision-making authority. Here's a framework I've developed for breaking the silence strategically.

Operational Truth-Sharing

Begin with honest transparency about operational conditions. Instead of saying "everything is on track" when timelines are tight, try "we're managing three risks that could affect our timeline—here's how we're addressing each one." This shares information without causing panic.

Example: Rather than presenting quarterly projections as certainties, acknowledge the assumptions underlying your forecasts and invite input on variables that could affect outcomes.

Strategic Uncertainty Acknowledgment

When dealing with truly uncertain strategic decisions, try making the uncertainty explicit. "We have strong reasons to believe this approach will work, but we're making this decision with incomplete information. Here's what we know, what we don't know, and how we'll learn as we implement."

Example: Priya began starting significant strategic discussions with "Here's what I'm certain about, what I'm uncertain about, and what questions I need your help thinking through." This shifted meetings from information delivery to collective problem-solving.

Selective Authority Distribution

Identify decisions you're making alone that could benefit from distributed intelligence. This isn't about consensus-building or avoiding accountability—it's about gaining information and perspectives that enhance decision quality.

Example: Sarah began delegating certain operational decisions entirely while maintaining clear parameters for escalation. This freed her capacity for strategic thinking while developing her team's decision-making capabilities.

Authentic Limitation Acknowledgment

Perhaps most importantly, practice admitting the limits of your expertise. "This touches on areas where others on the team have more experience than I do. Let me facilitate a conversation between the people with the most relevant knowledge."

This type of leadership boosts team confidence rather than diminishes it because it shows awareness of when to take charge and when to coordinate.

Example: Priya started naming the limits of her expertise in meetings: "I can assess the regulatory risk, but the engineering team understands the technical trade-offs better." Her team began bringing her into decisions earlier because they trusted she'd add value rather than override.

The Science Behind Leadership Silence

The costs of leadership silence extend beyond individual stress. Research across psychology, organizational behavior, and neuroscience reveals measurable damage from the patterns that high achievers develop to project invulnerability.

- **Leadership Loneliness.** The Harvard Business Review CEO Snapshot Survey found that 50% of CEOs feel lonely in their roles, and 61% believe this loneliness hinders their performance. A 2024 survey found 55% of CEOs reported mental health issues, including anxiety and burnout, a 24-percentage point increase from the previous year. Harvard research found loneliness has health effects comparable to smoking fifteen cigarettes daily.
- **The Cost of Emotional Suppression.** Alicia Grandey's research at Penn State University found that "surface acting," suppressing genuine emotions to display expected ones, leads to emotional exhaustion, burnout, insomnia, and reduced self-control. Leaders perform emotional labor at a frequency matching that of frontline service workers yet rarely acknowledge it. The mask itself becomes the source of exhaustion.

- **Barriers to Help-Seeking.** Pepperdine University research identified five barriers preventing high performers from seeking help: stigma, career consequences, organizational culture, structural isolation, and logistics. McLean Hospital and Harvard Medical School found 26% of executives report symptoms consistent with clinical depression, compared to 18% in the general workforce. Only 12% of CEOs have a formal coach.
- **The Psychological Safety Connection.** Amy Edmondson's Harvard Business School research established psychological safety as the primary predictor of team effectiveness. Her counterintuitive finding: Higher-performing hospital teams reported more errors because they felt safe admitting mistakes. When leaders cannot model uncertainty, team members keep critical information hidden.

Silence compounds rather than protects. What feels like strength becomes structural weakness, both for individuals and the organizations they lead.

Cross-Cultural Variations in Leadership Silence

The relationship between authority and vulnerability varies significantly across cultural contexts, and understanding these differences can inform more effective approaches to breaking professional silence:

- **American Leadership Culture:** Often emphasizes individual authority and decisive action, making strategic uncertainty feel risky. But this culture also values innovation and adaptability, which require precisely the kind of collective thinking that silence prevents.
- **European Leadership Models:** Generally, more comfortable with collaborative decision-making and distributed authority, but sometimes at the cost of decisive action when speed is required.
- **Scandinavian Approach:** The concept of *janteloven* (roughly: No one is better than anyone else) creates natural permission for

leaders to acknowledge limitations, but requires balancing humility with the clarity that teams need for effective action.

- **East Asian Leadership Traditions:** Often emphasize consensus-building and collective understanding, but formal hierarchy can sometimes prevent the open dialogue necessary for accessing that collective intelligence.

None of these approaches is universally better, but appreciating cultural context can assist leaders in adjusting their approach to breaking the silence in ways that suit their particular organizational and cultural environment.

What I Wish I'd Known: Professional Silence

The strongest leaders aren't those who bear the most weight alone, but those who build systems sturdy enough to support the weight together. Your job isn't to have all the answers, but to create conditions where the best answers can emerge from collective intelligence.

True *fællesskab*—genuine community—requires a kind of vulnerability that feels risky at first but ultimately creates more security than any individual display of strength ever could. Sometimes the most powerful thing a leader can say is "I don't know, but here's how we can figure it out together."

Most importantly, silence isn't a sign of strength—it's a barrier to the collaborative intelligence needed to solve complex challenges. The goal isn't to tell everything to everyone, but to identify what you're unnecessarily hiding and experiment with selective, strategic truth-sharing that boosts your effectiveness instead of weakening it.

Breaking the Silence Assessment

Identify one area where your silence might be limiting team effectiveness.

Operational Level Assessment:

- What operational challenges are you managing alone that others could help address?

- What resource constraints or timeline pressures are you buffering that your team could help solve?
- What implementation obstacles are you working around that would benefit from collective problem-solving?

Strategic Level Assessment:

- What strategic uncertainties are you carrying alone that would benefit from diverse perspectives?
- What market changes or competitive pressures are you analyzing independently that your team could help interpret?
- What aspects of the current strategy feel uncertain or risky?

Relational Level Assessment:

- How is your current approach to authority affecting team dynamics?
- What interpersonal challenges need addressing that you've been managing individually?
- Where do you need more support or different types of support?

Integration Questions:

- What would change if you shared one operational truth this week?
- Which strategic uncertainty might benefit from collective thinking?
- What would *fællesskab* look like in your specific context?

Remember: The goal isn't to share everything with everyone but to identify what you're carrying unnecessarily and to practice selective, strategic truth-sharing that boosts rather than harms your effectiveness.

Questions for Reflection

Transformational Question: "What truth, if spoken, would set you free?"

This isn't about confession or dramatic revelation. It's about recognizing the real situation you're handling on your own that could turn into a collective strength if approached thoughtfully.

Personal Awareness: What are you carrying alone that others could help you with? What truths are you protecting others from that might strengthen their capacity to contribute?

Systemic Thinking: How does your team or organization reward silence and punish vulnerability? What would change if truth-telling were truly safe and strategic?

Action-Oriented: Who is one person you could practice greater honesty with this week? What small truth could you share that might improve rather than complicate your working relationship?

Integration: Where else in your life do you perform strength when you actually need support? How might this pattern be affecting your relationships, health, or capacity for authentic connection?

From Carrying to Sharing

I am sitting at Søerne in Copenhagen, with runners passing by and people walking their dogs before heading to work. Priya sent me a message last night. Her team just successfully handled their first major regulatory challenge since our engagement began. Instead of presenting the challenge as something she had under control, she asked the team to think through the implications together. The result was a more creative solution than she could have come up with alone.

The strongest leaders aren't those who bear the most weight alone, but those who create systems strong enough to support the weight together. True *fællesskab* requires a level of vulnerability that initially feels risky but ultimately fosters more security than any individual display of strength ever could.

But what happens when that way of being becomes a way of life for the individual? When professional over-functioning becomes so ingrained that we lose the ability to recognize our own limits until our bodies force a reckoning? When does the silence of strength lead us directly to the edge of collapse? Chapter 3 answers those questions.

3 Living on the Edge of Collapse

How high performance turns into burnout, and how to recover before it's too late.

Twelve thirty on a Wednesday in Berlin's Mitte district, and the lunch crowd fills the sidewalk tables of Einstein Unter den Linden with conversations in four languages. The fall air has that scent that makes you want to linger over a meal while the autumn light slants through bare trees onto worn brick streets. Office workers emerge from nearby buildings with the purposeful energy of people who have ninety minutes to reset before afternoon meetings. Still, somehow the café maintains the unhurried atmosphere that makes Berlin feel different from other business capitals.

I'm here to meet Stefan, an automotive operations director, whose calendar shows three more meetings this afternoon, two calls tonight, and a weekend working session that his wife Anna has stopped questioning. But Stefan won't be talking about his schedule. He'll be talking about something more fundamental: the moment he realized he was three conversations away from complete breakdown, and how he learned to recognize the difference between sustainable pace and sophisticated self-destruction.

Stefan arrives exactly on time, which doesn't surprise me—German precision is legendary for good reason. What does surprise me is how he moves: the careful, measured steps of someone who has learned that rushing everywhere is actually getting him nowhere. He orders a simple coffee, no modifications, and settles into the chair across from me with the kind of presence that suggests he's been thinking about this conversation for weeks.

"Before we begin," he says in that direct way that bypasses small talk, "I need you to understand something. Last Tuesday, my son presented his school project on renewable energy. I missed it because I was in a meeting that could have been an email. When I got home, he had already gone to bed, but he left me a piece of cake. A piece of cake!"

He pauses, stirs his coffee slowly, and looks out at the street where people are navigating their lunch break with the unhurried rhythm that characterizes Berlin's approach to work-life integration.

"That's when I knew something fundamental had to change. I'm not the dad that gets leftover cake . . . I'm the dad who is there when it is made."

The Architecture of Breaking Points

What Stefan was discovering is what I learned during my own reckoning five years ago: Collapse follows predictable patterns. It's not random. It's not a weakness. It's the inevitable result of systems pushed beyond their sustainable limits. The automotive industry is transforming faster than anyone predicted: electric vehicles, autonomous systems, supply chain disruptions, and regulatory changes that reshape everything quarterly. As Operations Director, Stefan's job is to help his company navigate these changes while maintaining production targets, quality standards, and employee morale.

But here's what nobody mentions in leadership development programs: It's exhausting to remain confident and decisive when everything feels uncertain and unstable. The energy required to project competence while learning in real time, to maintain team morale while privately questioning strategic direction, to optimize operations while the entire industry undergoes fundamental transformation—this creates a particular kind of depletion that accumulates until the system can no longer function.

What I've discovered through my own experience and work with leaders is that high achievers often mistake the warning signs of approaching breakdown for the requirements of leadership. The sleepless nights, the constant availability, the feeling that everything depends on your personal attention—these aren't signs of commitment. They're symptoms of unsustainable system design.

The Collapse Continuum

To understand how sustainable high performance becomes an unsustainable breakdown, I've mapped what I call the Collapse Continuum: the predictable progression from optimization to crisis. Understanding these stages allows for course correction before a crisis becomes inevitable.

Stage 1: Optimization

This feels like peak performance. You're handling high demands with apparent ease, productivity is firm, and feedback is positive. Energy levels remain good, relationships are stable, and you feel in control of your responsibilities. The system operates efficiently, and there's even some buffer for unexpected demands.

But optimization contains the seeds of its own undoing. Success creates more opportunities, which generate more demands, which require more energy. The system begins operating closer to its limits without initially showing strain. For Stefan, this stage meant successfully implementing new quality protocols while managing supply chain disruptions, all while maintaining his reputation as the operations director who "always finds a way."

Warning signs: Slightly less sleep but feeling fine, minor increases in caffeine use, occasional irritability dismissed as everyday stress, fewer purely social activities, but nothing that feels concerning.

Stage 2: Acceleration

The pace increases, but performance remains high. You start needing external supports: caffeine to wake up, alcohol to wind down, constant stimulation to feel normal. Efficiency becomes crucial because the margin for error is shrinking, but results still meet or exceed expectations.

This is where Stefan found himself six months before our meeting—working later, traveling more frequently, and bringing work home mentally even when physically present. His team respected his dedication, his superiors praised his results, but professional demands were slowly crowding out his personal life.

Warning signs: Chronic minor health issues like headaches or digestive problems, relationship tensions that feel manageable but persistent, irritability over small things that used to roll off, difficulty being fully present during downtime, decreased enjoyment of previously pleasurable activities.

Stage 3: Strain

The foundation starts to show cracks. Decision-making becomes harder because cognitive resources are stretched thin. Creativity diminishes as mental energy goes toward maintaining basic function. You feel like you're working harder for less satisfaction, and others begin noticing changes in your behavior, mood, or effectiveness.

Stefan recognized this stage when he found himself snapping at his seven-year-old son for asking simple questions about homework, when colleagues mentioned that he seemed "different" in team meetings, and when Anna asked if everything was okay with increasing frequency. The work was getting done, but the person doing it was changing in ways that weren't sustainable.

Warning signs: Procrastination on essential tasks, cynicism about work that once excited you, frequent minor illnesses as the immune system weakens, conflicts with trusted colleagues or family members, difficulty concentrating on complex problems, and relying on systems and reminders for things you used to remember naturally.

Stage 4: Crisis

Something breaks—physically, emotionally, or professionally. This might be a health scare, a relationship crisis, a significant mistake at work, or simply the inability to continue at the current pace. The situation forces a reckoning with unsustainable patterns, but often when options are already limited.

For Stefan, the crisis came during a weekend planning session when he realized he couldn't remember the last time he'd had a conversation with Anna that wasn't about logistics, schedules, or household management. "I looked at my calendar and saw three weeks straight without a single evening at home before eight p.m. That's when I understood this wasn't a busy period—this had become my life."

Warning signs: Physical symptoms that can't be ignored (chest pain, severe headaches, panic attacks), major conflicts with essential relationships, significant performance issues despite increased effort, the feeling that you can't keep going but don't know how to stop.

Stage 5: Collapse

The system shuts down for protection. This might be physical illness, emotional breakdown, or simply the complete inability to maintain previous levels of function. Like that February morning for me, choice is removed from the equation—your body or mind enforces the limits you've been ignoring.

The crucial insight Stefan and I both learned is that collapse isn't failure—it's protection. When we refuse to respect our limits, our bodies and minds eventually enforce them for us. The goal isn't to prevent all breakdowns, but to recognize and respond to earlier stages before intervention requires a crisis.

Building Collapse Resilience

Understanding the Collapse Continuum is valuable only if it leads to practical changes in how you operate. Here are the strategies I've developed for building what I call "collapse resilience"—the ability to recognize and respond to warning signs before they become crises.

Early Warning Systems

Just as aircraft have multiple warning systems to prevent crashes, high-performing leaders need multiple warning systems to avoid collapse. These might include the following:

- **Physical Indicators:** Regular monitoring of sleep quality, energy patterns, and physical symptoms. Stefan began rating his energy level (1–10) each morning, which revealed patterns that a gradual decline had made invisible. When his average dropped below 6 for three consecutive days, it triggered systematic recovery protocols.

- **Emotional Indicators:** Weekly check-ins with trusted colleagues or family members who can observe changes in mood, patience, or emotional availability that you might not notice yourself. Anna became Stefan's early emotional warning system, with permission to call attention to changes in his presence or responsiveness.
- **Performance Indicators:** Tracking not just results but the effort required to achieve them. When tasks that used to feel manageable become difficult, that's information about approaching limits rather than personal weakness. Stefan noticed that quarterly planning, which used to energize him, had become something he dreaded and postponed.
- **Relational Indicators:** Monitoring the quality of connections with others. Isolation, irritability, or difficulty being present often precede other forms of breakdown. Stefan realized he was measuring success by tasks completed rather than relationships maintained.

Designing Recovery

Most high achievers are sophisticated about strategy, planning, and execution. Few are equally sophisticated about recovery. Yet recovery isn't the absence of work—it's a specific set of practices that restore capacity for high performance.

- **Micro recoveries:** Brief periods throughout the day that reset your nervous system. Two minutes of deep breathing between meetings, a short walk around the building, or simply looking out the window without mental activity. Stefan built five-minute buffers between all meetings for transition and reset.
- **Daily recoveries:** Structured practices that create a transition between high-intensity work and personal time. This might include exercise, meditation, reading, or any activity that engages different neural networks than those used for work. Stefan instituted a "shutdown ritual"—ten minutes of reviewing the day and setting intentions for tomorrow—that created psychological separation between work and home.
- **Weekly recoveries:** Longer periods that allow for deeper restoration. Research suggests that complete disconnection from work for at least twenty-four hours per week is necessary for preventing

cumulative stress. Stefan designated Saturday mornings as completely work-free time, which initially felt impossible but became non-negotiable.

- **Seasonal recoveries:** Extended periods that allow for reflection, perspective, and renewal of motivation. These aren't luxuries for high achievers—they're maintenance requirements for complex systems. Stefan began taking actual vacations where he didn't check email and discovered that the world continued functioning without his constant oversight.

The Preemptive Principle

The most effective approach to collapse prevention is preemptive: making changes while you still feel capable rather than waiting until you feel desperate. This requires overriding the high achiever's instinct to push to the limit.

Preemptive action is reducing travel before you feel overwhelmed, delegating responsibility before you feel overloaded, or taking time off before you feel exhausted. It requires what the Danes call *tillid*—trust that stepping back will ultimately serve your goals better than pushing forward.

Stefan's breakthrough came when he began treating his limits as strategic assets rather than obstacles to overcome. "I realized that my capacity wasn't unlimited, so I needed to deploy it strategically rather than reactively. This shift from endless pushing to intelligent pacing changed everything."

The Science Behind Burnout Progression

Burnout follows predictable biological and psychological patterns. Understanding the science helps leaders recognize warning signs before a crisis becomes inevitable.

- **WHO Classification.** In 2019, the World Health Organization classified burnout in ICD-11 as "a syndrome resulting from chronic workplace stress that has not been successfully managed," characterized by three dimensions: energy depletion, increased mental distance and cynicism, and reduced professional efficacy. This official recognition established burnout as an occupational phenomenon rather than an individual weakness.

- **The Four-Stage Biological Progression.** Research from Universidad Siglo 21 published in *Frontiers in Neuroscience* identified four distinct phases with measurable cortisol differences: Engaged (42% of workers), Strained (29%), Cynical (17%), and Burned-out (12%). Critically, cortisol levels increase during strained and cynical phases, then decline in burned-out individuals. The HPA axis literally exhausts itself, explaining the profound fatigue of late-stage burnout.
- **Executive Vulnerability.** A Deloitte C-Suite study found 70% of executives are so burned out that they're considering quitting for jobs that better support well-being, 82% of CEOs have experienced exhaustion indicative of burnout, and 96% feel their mental health has declined. The American Hospital Association found 71% of healthcare executives are concerned that burnout will affect their careers.
- **Early Warning Patterns.** Christina Maslach and Michael Leiter's research at UC Berkeley tracked employees over one year, finding that workers showing "inconsistent patterns," mismatched scores like high exhaustion but still engaged, were more likely to change status within a year. Workplace fairness emerged as the tipping point: At-risk workers who perceived unfairness moved toward burnout; those without this perception moved toward engagement.

The research reveals burnout as staged and predictable rather than sudden and random. This means intervention windows exist, but they close as the progression advances.

The Transformation Available in Crisis

While I don't recommend collapse as a growth strategy, I've observed that leaders who experience and properly integrate breakdown often emerge with capabilities they didn't possess before the crisis forced their evolution.

- **Enhanced Self-Awareness:** Operating at the edge of limits teaches you to recognize subtle internal signals—both yours and others'. Stefan developed what he calls "early detection systems" (like those covered earlier in this chapter) that allow him to course-correct before small stresses become significant problems.
- **Improved Emotional Intelligence:** Collapse forces honest evaluation of what's sustainable and what isn't. This painful clarity becomes the foundation for more intelligent choices about how to deploy energy and attention. Stefan became more skilled at reading team dynamics and individual stress levels, which made him more effective at preventing rather than managing problems.
- **More Profound Empathy:** Understanding your own vulnerability makes you more attuned to others' struggles. Leaders who have faced their limits often become more effective at supporting team members facing theirs. Stefan's team began bringing him concerns earlier because they trusted he would respond with understanding rather than pressure.
- **Systems Thinking:** Collapse reveals how interconnected your various life systems are. Work stress affects sleep quality, which affects decision-making, which affects relationships, which affects recovery, which involves work performance. Stefan learned to optimize for the whole system rather than individual components.

Cross-Cultural Approaches to Sustainable Pacing

Different cultures have developed various ideas about the relationship between effort and sustainability, and these approaches offer insights for individual practice:

- **German Engineering Mindset:** Emphasizes systematic maintenance and sustainable performance over time. Like a well-engineered machine, humans require regular maintenance to prevent breakdown. Stefan applied this engineering thinking to his own capacity management.

- **Scandinavian *Mådehold*:** The Danish concept of moderation—not as settling for less, but as building capacity for more. The most impressive achievements often come from sustainable pacing rather than heroic sprints.
- **Mediterranean Rhythm:** The integration of work and rest throughout the day and year, recognizing that different seasons require different approaches to effort and recovery.

Each approach offers insights, but the key is developing your own systematic approach to recognizing and respecting limits before they're enforced for you.

What I Wish I'd Known: Signs of Collapse

If I could go back to my younger self, the one who believed that 180 travel days a year was sustainable, who thought three hours of sleep was sufficient, who assumed that willpower could substitute for time, I would offer this counsel:

Your body is not the enemy of your ambition—it's the vehicle for it. When it sends signals of exhaustion, pain, or overwhelm, it's not trying to sabotage your success. It's trying to preserve your capacity for long-term achievement.

The warning signs of approaching collapse aren't character flaws to be overcome—they're information to be heeded. That difficulty falling asleep isn't just stress; it's your nervous system providing crucial feedback. That irritability with loved ones isn't just personality; it's emotional depletion demanding attention.

Most importantly, stepping back from the edge isn't giving up—it's a strategy. The leaders who sustain high performance over decades are not the ones who push through every limit, but the ones who respect their limits and design their lives accordingly.

That February morning taught me that collapse can be a teacher, if we're willing to listen to what it's trying to tell us. The goal isn't to prevent all struggle, but to distinguish between productive challenge and destructive overwhelm.

The Collapse Prevention Assessment

Take a moment to assess where you are on the Collapse Continuum honestly:

Stage 1: Optimization Indicators:

- Handling high demands with apparent ease
- Firm productivity and positive feedback
- Good energy levels and stable relationships
- Feeling in control of responsibilities

Stage 2: Acceleration Indicators:

- Needing external support (caffeine, alcohol, stimulation)
- Working longer hours but maintaining results
- Slightly less sleep, but feeling functional
- Minor increases in irritability or impatience

Stage 3: Strain Indicators:

- Decision-making feels more difficult
- Less creative or innovative thinking
- Working harder for the same or less satisfaction
- Others commenting on changes in behavior

Stage 4: Crisis Indicators:

- Physical symptoms that can't be ignored
- Major conflicts in meaningful relationships
- Significant performance issues despite increased effort
- Feeling unable to continue, but not knowing how to stop

Prevention Strategies:

- What early warning systems could you implement?
- What recovery protocols would be most beneficial?
- Where could you apply the preemptive principle?
- Who could serve as an external perspective on your stress levels?

Questions for Reflection

Transformational Question: "What could this breakdown be trying to teach you?"

This isn't about finding silver linings in suffering, but about extracting insight from difficulty. What capabilities might emerge from honestly confronting your limits? What strength might come from accepting rather than fighting your humanity?

Personal Awareness: What warning signs have you been ignoring? When do you feel closest to your edge? What does your body tell you about a sustainable pace that your mind might be overriding?

Systemic Thinking: How does your work environment normalize operating at unsustainable levels? What would true sustainability look like in your role, industry, or organization? What would need to change?

Action-Oriented: What would you stop doing immediately if you took your edge seriously? What boundaries would you set? What would you delegate, eliminate, or restructure?

Integration: How might slowing down in one area of your life create more capacity in others? Where could sustainable pacing improve rather than diminish your results?

What I Didn't Know Yet

I'm walking through Berlin's Tiergarten, where the afternoon light filters through trees that have learned to grow slowly and last for centuries. Stefan sent me a photo this morning—he and his son building a school science project together on a Wednesday evening, both of them grinning with glue on their fingers. "Home by six," his message read. "Turns out the company didn't collapse when I left at a reasonable hour."

The best leaders I know have learned that their job isn't to sacrifice themselves for their work, but to sustain themselves for their work. They've discovered that respecting their limits doesn't diminish their impact—it enhances it. They've understood that collapse isn't an occupational hazard to be endured, but a system failure to be prevented.

They've learned that sometimes the most powerful thing a leader can do is step back from the edge before being forced over it. Embrace the Danish meaning of *mådehold*. Moderation isn't about settling for less—it's about building capacity for more. The most impressive achievements often come from sustainable pacing, not heroic sprints.

But sustainable pacing is only possible when you understand what's really driving the unsustainable pace in the first place. What if the problem isn't time management or schedule optimization? What if it's something more fundamental about how we think about energy itself?

That was the question I was wrestling with in 2020. Within a few years, that question would become more complex. Artificial intelligence would arrive and change the nature of the system itself—not just making leaders busier, but fundamentally shifting what leadership required. The unsustainable pace wasn't just about too many meetings or too little time. It was about too many decisions, too much information, too many options to evaluate. AI would make all of that exponentially harder.

The leaders who would navigate that shift successfully wouldn't be the ones who got better at time management. They'd be the ones who understood what was actually breaking inside them—and redesigned their relationship with work before the system broke them completely.

4 Energy Management in the Modern Organization

Energy as the real asset, and how to reclaim time, clarity, and bandwidth in high-stakes roles.

The coffee shop in Munich's Schwabing district has its own rhythm this afternoon—espresso machine hissing, conversations in three languages overlapping, the sound of wooden chairs scraping against old floors. I'm here early for my meeting with Klaus, the fintech founder who reached out through a VC we both know: "I'm winning at work and losing at home, and I can't figure out how to do both anymore."

Klaus's movements are deliberate. Careful, measured steps of someone who has learned that rushing everywhere is getting him nowhere. He orders a simple coffee, no modifications. He settles into the chair across from me with the kind of exhausted presence that suggests he's been running on reserve capacity for months.

"Before we begin," he says in that direct German way that bypasses small talk, "I need you to understand something. Last Thursday evening,

I was reviewing board materials on my phone during dinner. My wife Anna asked me to put it away, so I did. Later that night, I picked up my phone and found three messages from Felix, my eleven-year-old. The first one: 'Can you help with my science project?' Sent at 4:47 p.m. Second one: 'Dad?' at 6:23 p.m. Third one: 'It's ok, I did it myself' at 8:11 p.m."

He pauses, stirs his coffee slowly, the spoon clinking against the ceramic. Through the window, the sound of trams passing punctuates the street noise.

"I was in the same house as him the entire time. I just never saw the messages because I was in back-to-back calls, then email, then board prep. When I finally read them at 10:30 that night, he was already asleep. I realized I'd become the kind of father whose son has learned to stop asking for help."

"That's when I knew something fundamental had to change. Not my schedule—I've tried rearranging that a dozen times. Not my priorities—I've reorganized those more than my son has changed his favorite hairstyle. Something deeper. The way I think about energy itself."

The Hidden Architecture of Energy

What Klaus was discovering is what I learned during my own reckoning five years ago: Energy management isn't just about time allocation or task prioritization. It's about understanding the hidden architecture of how we spend our most precious resource—our capacity for presence, attention, and authentic engagement.

In Denmark, we have a concept called *arbejdsglæde*—literally "work joy"—that captures something the productivity industry completely misses. It's not about finding passion in your work or achieving work-life balance. It's about sustainable engagement that enhances rather than depletes your capacity for all the other things that matter.

The American approach to energy management typically focuses on optimization: how to squeeze more output from the same input, how to hack your way to higher performance, how to find the perfect morning routine or productivity system. But *arbejdsglæde* suggests something different—that work, when appropriately aligned, should generate energy that spills over into the rest of your life.

The German approach, which Klaus was unconsciously following, emphasizes systematic efficiency and continuous improvement. But even the most sophisticated systems can become energy drains when they're optimized for the wrong variables. Klaus had built an incredibly efficient machine for producing business results, but he'd forgotten to design it in ways that sustained the human being operating it.

Understanding Your Energy Architecture

Beyond the simple categorization of physical, mental, and emotional energy lies something more nuanced: the architecture of when and how different types of work feel most natural. We each have what I call "energy rhythms"—predictable patterns of when other kinds of engagement feel effortless versus exhausting.

Morning Energy Architecture

Often characterized by high cognitive capacity, creative thinking, and complex problem-solving abilities. Morning is when your brain's executive function operates at peak efficiency, making it ideal for strategic work, difficult decisions, and tasks requiring deep focus.

Klaus discovered that his most energizing work—the strategic thinking that had built his company—was being crowded out by reactive tasks that felt urgent but weren't important. His mornings, which should have been protected for high-level thinking, were consumed by email, quick decisions, and "urgent" meetings that drained his capacity for everything else.

Midday Energy Architecture

Typically midday is optimal for collaborative work, relationship building, and communication-intensive tasks. Your social processing capabilities are often strongest during these hours, making it the ideal time for team meetings, client conversations, and collaborative problem-solving.

"I realized I was scheduling my most important strategic discussions during my lowest-energy time slots," Klaus reflected months later. "Board meetings at the end of fourteen-hour days, client presentations when

I was already depleted, team planning sessions when everyone was running on caffeine and stress. No wonder our decision-making felt so difficult."

Evening Energy Architecture

Generally evening is suited for reflection, planning, and administrative tasks that require less intensive cognitive load. This is often when your brain naturally shifts toward integration and processing, making it ideal for reviewing the day, setting intentions for tomorrow, and handling routine tasks.

The breakthrough for Klaus came when he began treating his energy architecture as seriously as his financial budget. "I stopped scheduling meetings based on calendar availability and started scheduling them based on energy compatibility," he explained. "Client meetings during my high-relationship energy times, strategic thinking during my peak cognitive hours, and administrative tasks during natural low-energy periods."

Guarding Your Energy with the Reflect/Respond/React Framework

One of the most energy-intensive patterns Klaus and I both recognized was the constant state of reactivity that modern leadership seems to require. Email, Slack messages, urgent requests, crisis management—the contemporary leader spends most of their time responding to external demands rather than creating from internal intention.

But sustainable leadership requires moving through a different sequence, what I call the Reflect/Respond/React framework.

Reflect First

Before acting, pause long enough to understand what's needed. What outcome are you trying to create? What's the most intelligent response rather than the most immediate one? This isn't about slowing down—it's about acting from choice rather than compulsion.

Klaus began building what he called "reflection buffers" into his day—sixty seconds between meetings to consider what had just happened and what was about to happen, five minutes at the beginning of each day to set intentions rather than just reviewing tasks, ten minutes at the end of each day to process rather than just plan.

Respond Strategically

Act from intention rather than impulse. Consider not just what needs to be done, but who's best positioned to do it, when it needs to happen, and how it connects to larger objectives. Strategic response often means doing less but accomplishing more.

"I discovered that about half of what felt urgent actually wasn't," Klaus says. "When I started asking 'What happens if we don't do this right now?' the answer was often 'Nothing significant.' That freed up enormous amounts of energy for work that mattered."

Skip Reaction

Bypass the emotional urgency that creates poor decisions and energy drain. Skipping a reaction doesn't mean being unresponsive—it means responding from clarity rather than chaos, from wisdom rather than worry.

This framework transformed Klaus's experience of leadership from constant crisis management to strategic orchestration. "I stopped feeling like I was being acted upon by external forces and started feeling like I was acting from internal strength," he reflects.

The Energy Ecosystem Model

Working with leaders across different industries and cultures, I've developed what I call the Energy Ecosystem Model—a way of understanding how various types of energy interact and influence each other within organizations.

The model distinguishes between two dimensions: individual energy (how you personally generate and spend capacity) and collective energy (how energy moves through teams and organizations). Both connect to the energy architectures we explored earlier. Your personal sustainability depends on managing your own energy types, but your leadership impact depends on understanding how energy flows through the systems you influence. Let me break down each dimension.

Individual energy types include the following:

- **Generative Energy:** Work that creates capacity rather than consuming it. This includes activities that align with your strengths, contribute to meaningful outcomes, and leave you feeling more alive rather than depleted. For Klaus, this was strategic thinking about product development and company vision.
- **Transactional Energy:** Necessary activities that are energy-neutral when managed efficiently. This includes routine communication, administrative tasks, and maintenance activities that keep systems running smoothly. The key is preventing these from expanding into generative energy time slots.
- **Depleting Energy:** Work that consistently drains more energy than it provides. This might include activities that conflict with your values, require skills you don't enjoy using, or involve consistently complex relationships. The goal isn't to eliminate all depleting work, but to minimize it and recover afterward.

Collective energy patterns include the following:

- **Team Energy Synchronization:** Understanding when your team operates at peak collective capacity versus when individual energy management is more critical. Klaus learned that his team's energy patterns were different from his own and optimizing for collective rather than individual energy often produced better results.
- **Organizational Energy Flow:** How energy moves through systems, gets blocked, or gets amplified. Klaus discovered that specific meetings consistently drained everyone involved, while others left people feeling energized and aligned, and understanding these patterns allowed for systematic improvements in how work got done.
- **Cultural Energy Norms:** How different cultures approach the relationship between effort and sustainability. Klaus's company served clients across multiple continents, and understanding cultural differences in energy management improved both team dynamics and client relationships.

We'll return to mapping your personal energy architecture in the assessment later in this chapter. For now, consider when you typically feel most capable of complex thinking versus collaborative work.

Addressing Decision Fatigue in an AI Age with the Decision Protection Protocol

I started seeing a new pattern with my clients in early 2024: leaders who'd successfully automated parts of their work but somehow ended up more exhausted than before.

Marcus was typical. At 56, a CFO at a manufacturing company, he'd adopted artificial intelligence tools faster than most of his peers. Financial reports that used to take his team two days now took twenty minutes. Board prep that consumed his Fridays happened overnight.

"I got ninety minutes back in my day," he told me when we met in Copenhagen. "Maybe two hours."

"How are you feeling?" I asked.

He looked confused. "Productive. More efficient than I've been in years."

But his executive assistant had reached out first. Marcus was working later, not earlier. She'd found him at 7 p.m. reviewing AI-generated analyses of scenarios that hadn't even been proposed yet.

When I asked what he was doing with the time he'd saved, Marcus paused. "The AI can run more scenarios, so I review them. It can analyze more markets, so I check them. It can model more outcomes, so I evaluate them." He even sounded like a robot . . .

"You automated the easy parts," I said, "and filled the space with more of the hard parts."

He sat back. "I thought I was supposed to use the time to do more."

"What if you used it to think better?"

Marcus had fallen into what Klaus and I would later recognize as the automation trap—technology made specific tasks more efficient. Still, without a decision protection protocol, he simply filled the recovered time with exponentially more decisions to make. The tools got faster. His cognitive capacity didn't.

What Marcus needed wasn't better AI tools. He needed a systematic approach to deciding what deserved his attention.

That's precisely what the Decision Protection Protocol addresses. One of the most energy-intensive aspects of modern leadership is decision fatigue—the depletion that comes from making countless small choices throughout the day. Klaus, Marcus, and I developed what we now call the Decision Protection Protocol:

- **Decision Batching:** Group similar decisions together and handle them during specific time blocks rather than scattered throughout the day. Klaus began batching all personnel decisions into Tuesday morning meetings, all client decisions into Thursday planning sessions, and all operational decisions into Monday reviews. Marcus took a similar approach with financial approvals—Wednesdays only—which freed the rest of his week from constant budget interruptions.
- **Decision Delegation:** Identify decisions you're making that others could make with clear parameters. This isn't about avoiding responsibility—it's about deploying decision-making capacity strategically. Klaus created decision-making frameworks that allowed his team to handle routine choices without escalation. Marcus set approval thresholds that let his directors resolve anything under a certain budget without his input.
- **Decision Elimination:** Question whether certain decisions need to be made at all. Klaus discovered that many of the choices consuming his mental energy were non-decisions—situations where any reasonable option would work fine. Marcus stopped deliberating over vendor selections and travel bookings where the difference between options was negligible. Both were spending energy trying to optimize between equally good alternatives.
- **Decision Timing:** Make important decisions when your cognitive capacity is highest rather than when external pressure is greatest. Klaus stopped making significant strategic decisions at the end of long days and started protecting morning time for high-stakes choices as he was sharpest then, as revealed in his Energy Architecture. Marcus

moved his board prep from Friday afternoons to Tuesday mornings—same work, dramatically better output.

This protocol reduced Klaus's experience of decision fatigue while improving the quality of his decision-making. "I realized I was treating every choice as equally important," he reflects. "When I started triaging decisions based on impact and urgency, everything became clearer."

The Science Behind Sustainable Engagement

Research in organizational psychology and neuroscience provides essential insights into why traditional approaches to productivity often backfire for high-performing leaders:

- **Attention Residue:** When you switch between tasks without proper closure, part of your attention remains stuck on the previous task. This creates cognitive interference that reduces performance on subsequent work. Klaus learned to make "transition rituals"—a short walk between meetings, three deep breaths before opening a new project, or simply closing all browser tabs and starting fresh—that helped his brain entirely shift between different types of work.
- **Ultradian Rhythms:** Your brain naturally cycles between periods of high focus and restoration approximately every 90–120 minutes throughout the day. Working with these rhythms rather than against them dramatically improves both performance and sustainability. The practical application is simple: Schedule focused work in 90-minute blocks with short breaks between them. Some leaders use timers; others learn to recognize their natural attention fade. The break doesn't need to be long—five minutes of movement, a brief conversation, or stepping outside—just enough to let your brain reset before the next cycle.
- **Social Energy Dynamics:** Your energy level significantly affects the energy of people around you. When leaders operate from

depletion, it creates organizational stress that compounds individual problems. When leaders model sustainable engagement, it creates permission for others to work more intelligently.

- **Recovery Science:** Different types of work require different types of recovery. Mental work requires physical movement, social work requires solitude, and creative work requires routine activities. Understanding these patterns allows for strategic restoration rather than generic "rest."

Cross-Cultural Approaches to Energy Management

Working with Klaus and other leaders across different cultural contexts has revealed interesting variations in how different societies approach the relationship between effort and sustainability:

- **German Systems Thinking:** Emphasizes systematic approaches to efficiency and maintenance. Like Klaus, German leaders often excel at building sophisticated systems but sometimes optimize for the wrong things. The strength is in systematic thinking; the opportunity is in applying that systems mindset to humans rather than just mechanical efficiency.
- **Scandinavian *Arbejdsglæde*:** The integration of joy and work, viewing sustainable engagement as both a personal and organizational responsibility. This approach recognizes that depleted leaders create depleted cultures, while energized leaders create energized teams.
- **American Optimization Culture:** Focuses on individual performance enhancement and productivity maximization. This creates high achievement potential but often at the cost of sustainable rhythms. The strength is in ambitious thinking; the opportunity is in applying that ambition to sustainability rather than just intensity.
- **Asian Relational Balance:** Views energy as flowing between people rather than being purely individual. Leaders in this tradition read team energy carefully and adjust their own output to maintain

collective equilibrium. The strength is in attunement to group dynamics; the opportunity is in balancing harmony with individual sustainability.

Each approach offers insights, but the key is developing your own systematic approach to energy management that works within your specific cultural and organizational context.

The Science Behind Energy and Decision-Making

The relationship between cognitive energy, decision quality, and recovery is among the most robust findings in behavioral science. Leaders who ignore these patterns pay measurable costs.

- **Decision Fatigue in High-Stakes Settings.** Shai Danziger's study at Columbia Business School analyzed 1,112 parole decisions by Israeli judges and found that the probability of a favorable ruling dropped from approximately 65% at the start of a session to nearly 0% at the end. After food breaks, favorable rulings rebounded to 65%. Featured in Kahneman's *Thinking, Fast and Slow*, this demonstrates that depleted decision-makers default to safer, easier choices rather than optimal ones.
- **Cumulative Cognitive Costs.** Harvard Business School research, conducted with Danish collaborators, analyzed 2 million standardized tests, and found that for every hour later in the day, test performance decreased by 0.9 standard deviations. A 20- to 30-minute break improved performance by 1.7 standard deviations. Mental resources deplete predictably over a regular workday.
- **Ultradian Performance Rhythms.** Nathaniel Kleitman's research at the University of Chicago documented that human bodies move through 90- to 120-minute cycles of varying alertness during both sleep and waking hours. Physiological measures, including heart rate, hormonal levels, and brain-wave activity, increase during the first 90 minutes, then decline, with the body naturally requiring recovery periods of 15–20 minutes after each cycle.

- **The Micro-Break Dividend.** A meta-analysis of twenty-two studies published in PLOS ONE found that micro-breaks had significant effects, boosting vigor and reducing fatigue. Harvard Business School research on fruit harvesters over 9,832 shifts found that breaks taken earlier in the day were more beneficial, and activities unrelated to work were most restorative. Recovery isn't weakness; it's strategic performance management with quantifiable returns.

Energy management isn't a soft science or wellness culture. It's applied cognitive neuroscience with direct implications for leadership effectiveness.

Using Energy for a New Perspective on Leadership

Six months after our first conversation, Klaus had fundamentally transformed his relationship with energy management. The changes weren't dramatic or revolutionary—they were incremental, yet systematic and sustainable.

"I started treating my energy like I treat our company's budget," Klaus explains. "Tracking it, allocating it, investing it in high-return activities, and protecting it from unnecessary expenditure. The parallels were remarkable."

The most significant change was in how Klaus structured his days. "I moved from reactive scheduling to strategic scheduling. Instead of fitting meetings into available time slots, I started fitting meetings into compatible energy slots. Board meetings during my peak strategic thinking time, client calls during my highest social energy, and administrative work during natural low-energy periods."

But the more profound transformation was in Klaus's understanding of leadership itself. "I realized that my job wasn't to solve every problem personally, but to create conditions where problems could be solved efficiently by the right people at the right time. This shift from individual heroics to systematic effectiveness changed everything."

The impact extended beyond Klaus to his entire team. "When I stopped operating from depletion, my team stopped feeling like they needed to compensate for my stress. They started bringing me solutions instead of just problems. They began taking initiative instead of waiting for direction. The organizational energy completely shifted."

Perhaps most importantly, the changes affected Klaus's relationship with his son. "I realized that being present for the big moments requires being energetically available, not just physically present. When I started protecting my energy, I had more capacity for the people and experiences that matter most."

Today, Klaus's company continues to grow rapidly, but from a foundation of sustainable engagement rather than unsustainable intensity. "I learned that the goal isn't to eliminate all energy expenditure," he reflects, "but to spend energy on things that generate more energy than they consume."

What I Wish I'd Known: Energy as Leadership Capital

If I could go back and tell my younger self one thing about energy management, it would be this: Your energy isn't just your personal resource to optimize—it's leadership capital that affects everyone around you.

When you operate from sustainable abundance, you create psychological safety for your team to dare take risks, share ideas, and bring their best thinking to complex problems. When you're reactive and depleted, you create an environment where people play it safe, avoid difficult conversations, and focus more on managing your stress than solving actual problems.

The question isn't just "How can I manage my energy better?" but "What kind of energy am I creating for the people around me?" This shift from individual optimization to collective impact changes everything about how you approach energy management.

Your energy state becomes your team's weather system. When you're scattered, they become scattered. When you're reactive, they become cautious. When you're depleted, they become conservative. But when you're operating from abundance, they become innovative. When you're present, they become engaged. When you're strategic, they become creative.

The Energy Architecture Assessment

Take a moment to map your own energy architecture and identify opportunities for improvement.

Personal Energy Mapping:

- When during the day do you feel most mentally sharp and capable of complex thinking?
- When do you have the most capacity for collaborative work and relationship building?
- When do you naturally feel more reflective and suited for planning or administrative tasks?
- What types of work consistently energize you versus drain you?

Current Energy Allocation:

- How much of your peak energy time is spent on generative versus transactional work?
- What percentage of your day is spent in reactive versus strategic mode?
- How often do you schedule essential decisions during your highest cognitive capacity times?

Energy Ecosystem Analysis:

- What patterns do you notice in your team's collective energy?
- How does your energy state affect the people around you?
- What organizational practices consistently generate energy versus deplete it?

Strategic Improvements:

- What's one change you could make this week to align your schedule with your energy architecture better?
- Where could you apply the Reflect/Respond/React framework?
- What decisions could you batch, delegate, eliminate, or time more strategically?

Questions for Reflection

Transformational Question: "What if less is more?"

This question challenges one of the deepest assumptions of high-achievement culture: that more effort, more hours, and more intensity automatically lead to better results. But what if sustainable excellence requires strategic subtraction? What if the most critical leadership skill is knowing what not to do?

Consider this possibility: The breakthrough you're looking for might not come from adding something new to your approach, but from removing something that's been draining your capacity for everything else.

Personal Awareness: When are you at your energetic best? What patterns can you identify about what drains versus energizes you? What does your energy tell you about alignment with your strengths and values?

Systemic Thinking: How does your organization measure and reward energy expenditure versus energy sustainability? What would change if energy were valued like a budget—with careful attention to ROI, strategic allocation, and sustainable practices?

Action-Oriented: What would you eliminate this week to create space for what truly energizes you? How will you protect your peak energy times? What reactive patterns could be interrupted with reflection?

Integration: How might managing your energy differently change your presence in relationships and personal commitments? When you're operating from abundance rather than depletion, how does that change your capacity for patience, curiosity, and genuine connection with the people you care about most?

From Busy to Present

As I finished writing this chapter, Klaus sent me a message—a photo of him and Felix working together on a new school project, both focused and present, no phones in sight except the one taking the picture. "Home by six has become the norm," his message read. "Amazing what's possible when you stop confusing busy with important."

Energy management isn't just about professional effectiveness—it's about showing up authentically in all the contexts that matter to you. When you're operating from abundance rather than depletion, it changes your capacity for patience, curiosity, and genuine connection with everyone around you.

But energy management alone isn't enough when the fundamental structure of your life is designed around unsustainable assumptions about what it means to be successful. What happens when professional over-functioning begins to erode the very relationships that make achievement meaningful? What's the real cost when work becomes not just a priority but the only priority that feels safe to prioritize?

5 The Other Divorce

When professional competence becomes a refuge from personal presence.

The marble table in the Aker Brygge café feels cold against my forearms—that eerie chill of stone that never quite warms to human contact, no matter how long you sit. I'm waiting for Anders, absently running my thumb along the edge of my coffee cup, feeling where the porcelain lip has been worn smooth by thousands of previous mouths, a bit off-putting and amazing at the same time. The weight of it is heavier than necessary, substantial in a way that suggests quality without needing to announce it.

Across from me, a woman is methodically tearing her croissant into precise pieces, placing each fragment on a napkin before eating it. There's something meditative in the repetition—tear, place, eat, repeat—as though she's buying time before returning to whatever awaits her in the glass tower visible through the café window. The paper napkin makes a soft sound each time she sets down another piece, and I find myself unconsciously matching my breathing to her rhythm.

I find myself in Oslo more often than I expected when I started this work. The city has a clear quality to it—all steel and glass and efficiency on the surface, but underneath there's this current of something older, more complex. You can feel it in the weight of history these streets carry, in the way modern consulting towers rise from cobblestone that remembers different eras entirely, in the contrast between smooth corporate marble and rough ancient stone.

Anders is in his early forties, dressed in the understated way that Nordic professionals have perfected—quality without flash. When we shake hands, his grip is firm, but his palm is slightly damp, and I notice how he immediately reaches for the napkin to dry his hands before ordering. Small tells of stress beneath the composed surface.

"I apologize for being exactly on time," he says with a grin, as he is often slightly late, which is such an odd thing to apologize for that I find myself smiling. "My daughter called as I was leaving the office. Her university application essay. She wanted my opinion on which direction to take it."

He orders an espresso, no sugar, and as he settles into the chair, I notice how he touches everything with deliberate precision—adjusts the saucer, straightens the spoon, aligns the cup handle. The kind of careful attention that people give to small objects when their minds are overwhelmed by larger concerns. A way to distract the mind.

"I told her what she had chosen was excellent, which it was. And then she asked me if I had read what she sent or just skimmed it. She could tell I was distracted, even on the phone. This is what I've come to talk to you about."

The Professional Refuge

Anders works as a management strategy consultant for one of the Big Five strategy consulting firms—the kind of role that exists to solve problems nobody else wants to touch. When the senior partners have a difficult client, Anders handles the relationship. When two project teams conflict, Anders brokers the peace. When a primary account threatens to leave, Anders flies to Helsinki, Stockholm, or Copenhagen to smooth things over.

It's the ultimate "fixer" position, and Anders has built a reputation for being unflappable, diplomatic, and practical. He's the person who makes impossible situations manageable, who translates between competing interests, who finds solutions when everyone else sees only problems.

"I'm very good at my job," he tells me, stirring his espresso slowly. "Perhaps too good. My partners depend on me. My colleagues appreciate me. Our clients trust me. I receive excellent reviews, and my compensation reflects my value."

He pauses, looking out at the street where business professionals move with purpose in what is Oslo's prime business district.

"But my daughter doesn't trust me anymore. Not really. She asks my opinion because she thinks she should, but I can hear in her voice that she's not expecting me to be present for the answer. And my ex-wife . . . well, there's a reason she's my ex-wife. She used to say I was having an affair with my mind, my competence, 'like a narcissistic a-hole.' At the time, I thought she was being dramatic and unfair. Now I understand she was being precise."

What Anders was describing is one of the most painful patterns I've encountered in my work with leaders—the way professional competence can become a refuge from the vulnerable, uncertain work of intimate relationships. When you're very good at solving problems, it's tempting to spend all your time in contexts where your expertise is valued and to avoid the contexts where being fully human requires admitting you don't have all the answers.

"At work, I know what to do," Anders continues. "When the partners ask me to handle something, I have frameworks, experience, and diplomatic skills. I can read the room, understand the dynamics, craft solutions. But when my daughter asks me about her essay, or wants to talk about her anxiety about university, or needs help with a conflict with her friends . . . I don't know what to do. I give advice, try to solve the problem, and offer my analysis. And I can see her pulling away, disappointed that I'm being a consultant when she needs a father."

This is the subtle tragedy of the absent leader—not someone who works too many hours or travels too much, though Anders did both. It's someone who has learned to feel safe and competent in professional contexts while struggling to show up authentically in personal relationships. They don't bring work intensity home—they hide from home's intensity in work.

Ro and the Certainty-Connection Paradox

In Norway, they have a word that captures something essential about this challenge: *ro*. It translates roughly as "calm" or "tranquility," but it means something more profound—a quality of centered presence that isn't dependent on having answers or solving problems. *Ro* is the opposite of reactive problem-solving. It's the capacity to be still and present with whatever is happening, without needing to fix or change it.

Anders had plenty of competence but almost no *ro*. Every situation was something to analyze, every conversation an opportunity to demonstrate his expertise, every relationship a problem to solve. He couldn't just be present because presence without productivity felt like failure.

"My daughter once told me something that I didn't understand at the time," Anders shared. "She said, 'Far, sometimes I don't need you to have an answer. I just need you to be worried with me.' I thought she was asking me to be ineffective. What I didn't understand is that she was asking me to be human."

This is what I've developed through my work with leaders who struggle with this pattern—not a system for better time management or work-life balance, but a framework for understanding what authentic presence requires and why it's so difficult for people who have built their identity around professional competence.

During our second session, I introduced Anders to the Certainty-Connection Paradox. It's a simple but powerful framework for understanding why professional competence can interfere with intimate relationships.

In professional contexts, competence is demonstrated through certainty. You're valued because you have answers, provide solutions, and offer expertise. Clients don't hire consultants to hear "I don't know." Partners don't promote people who frequently express uncertainty. Boards don't reward leaders who admit confusion.

But in intimate relationships, connection often requires uncertainty. Your daughter doesn't need you to solve her essay problem—she needs you to be curious about her thinking. Your partner doesn't want you to fix their difficult day—they want you to be present with their experience. Your friends don't need your analysis—they need your authenticity.

The paradox is this: The very skills that make you effective at work can make you unavailable at home. And the more successful you become professionally, the more tempting it is to spend time in contexts where your competence is valued and avoid contexts where being fully present requires admitting you don't have the answers.

Anders sat with this framework for a moment, his espresso growing cold.

"This explains something I've been feeling but couldn't articulate," he finally said. "At work, I feel valuable because I know what to do. At home, I feel uncertain because I often don't know what my daughter needs from me. I've been unconsciously spending more time where I feel competent and less time where I feel confused. I thought I was being strategic with my limited energy. What I was doing was abandoning my daughter in favor of my professional identity."

He paused, and I could see something shifting in his expression.

"That's not the father I want to be. That's not the person I want to be."

The Overfunctioning Pattern

As we continued working together, I introduced Anders to a second framework that helped illuminate why competence becomes refuge. It's the Overfunctioning Pattern, and it's particularly common among people in roles that require constant problem-solving.

Overfunctioning looks like helpfulness but functions as avoidance. You're constantly scanning for problems to solve, situations to improve, and people to help. At work, this is rewarded as initiative and leadership. But in intimate relationships, it prevents the kind of vulnerable reciprocity that creates actual connection.

When you're always in the helper role, you never have to be in the vulnerable position of needing help. When you're always solving other people's problems, you don't have to acknowledge your own uncertainties. When you're always competent, you don't have to risk being seen as merely human.

"That's what I do, constantly," Anders said. "At home, I'm constantly trying to optimize everything. I turn dinner conversations into learning opportunities. I give my daughter coaching when she needs comfort. I offer my ex-wife advice about her career when she's just trying to share her experience. I thought I was being helpful. What I was doing was maintaining distance through competence."

The Overfunctioning Pattern creates a "competence barrier"—an invisible wall you build with your expertise that protects you from the vulnerability of intimate relationships while appearing to be generous engagement.

This pattern is particularly insidious because it looks virtuous. You appear helpful, supportive, and engaged. But you're using your competence to avoid the uncertain terrain of authentic emotional presence.

The Three-Minute Presence Practice

Here's what I asked Anders to try, and what I suggest for anyone recognizing this pattern.

When someone you care about shares something with you—a challenge, a feeling, an experience—before responding with advice or solutions, take three full breaths and ask yourself:

> "What does this person need from me right now? Do they need my expertise, or do they need my presence?"

Then try one of these responses instead of immediately solving:

- "Tell me more about that."
- "How are you feeling about it?"
- "What's most difficult about this for you?"
- "I don't have an answer, but I'm here with you in figuring it out."

Notice what happens in your body when you resist the urge to be useful. Notice the discomfort of not having a solution to offer. Notice how the other person responds to presence rather than performance.

This practice feels impossibly simple when you read it, but surprisingly difficult when you try it. Your mind will immediately want to offer analysis, generate solutions, and demonstrate competence. That urge is the overfunctioning pattern trying to maintain the competence barrier.

The practice isn't about becoming passive or unhelpful. It's about learning to discern when people need your expertise and when they need your humanity—and being brave enough to offer the latter even when it feels less valuable than the former.

Six Weeks of Imperfect Practice

Anders implemented this presence practice with what he called "humbling inconsistency." Some days, he could be present without an agenda. Other days, he defaulted to consultant mode before catching himself. The work of changing ingrained patterns is not linear.

But about six weeks into practicing presence, Anders had an experience that shifted something fundamental. His daughter called him, clearly upset about a conflict with her flat mate. Anders felt his consulting mind activating—analyzing the dynamics, preparing diplomatic solutions, mentally drafting the perfect email his daughter could send.

Instead, he took three breaths and asked, "How are you feeling about all this?"

What followed was a forty-minute conversation where Anders mostly listened. His daughter talked through her hurt, her confusion about whether she'd done something wrong, and her worry about the living situation. Anders asked questions out of genuine curiosity rather than strategic information gathering. He shared a story about his own difficult roommate in graduate school—not as a lesson but as a connection. He admitted he didn't know what she should do, but he trusted her capacity to figure it out.

At the end of the call, his daughter said something that Anders later told me was the most meaningful thing she'd said to him in years:

> "Thanks, Dad. That really helped."
>
> "But I didn't do anything," Anders said to me later, still puzzled. "I didn't solve her problem. I didn't even offer advice."
>
> "Exactly," I said. "You were just present. And presence is what she needed."

This experience began to shift Anders's fundamental understanding of value. Being helpful wasn't always about having solutions. Maybe presence itself was a form of help, possibly the most essential form.

The Science Behind Work and Relationships

The collision between professional demands and intimate connection isn't anecdotal—decades of research document how competence at work can systematically erode presence at home.

- **Crossover Effects.** University of Georgia research followed 172 newlywed couples across four years and found significant crossover effects: When individuals experience high workloads, their partners show greater declines in marital satisfaction at subsequent time points. University of Iowa research identified "psychological withdrawal" as the mechanism. Work stress causes emotional absence even when physically present.

- **The Promotion Divorce Premium.** Stockholm University and Uppsala University researchers analyzing thirty years of Swedish data found that female CEOs who were married at the time of promotion are more than twice as likely to be divorced three years later than their male counterparts. The researchers note divorces concentrated in gender-traditional couples where economic and status balance became disrupted by the woman's advancement.
- **Workaholism and Marriage.** Bryan Robinson's research at UNC found divorce rates 40% higher among workaholics, with marriages involving at least one workaholic spouse nearly twice as likely to end in divorce. Erasmus University Rotterdam's research on 168 dual-earner couples confirmed that workaholism leads to work-family conflict, reduced partner support, and decreased relationship satisfaction for both partners.
- **Predictive Patterns of Disconnection.** John and Julie Gottman's forty years of research at the University of Washington studying 3,000 couples found that they can predict divorce with over 90% accuracy based on interaction patterns. Stonewalling, withdrawal from connection when emotions run high, emerged as one of the "Four Horsemen" predicting relationship failure. 85% of Stonewallers are men, and patterns of disengagement show 80% stability over three years.

Professional excellence and relational presence operate on different systems. Success in one domain doesn't transfer automatically to the other, and may actively interfere with it.

The Energy Paradox of Presence

One of the most counterintuitive insights Anders discovered through this practice was the Energy Paradox of Presence: Being authentically present requires less energy than performing competence, even though it initially feels more vulnerable, even draining as you are holding back.

When you're constantly performing competence—analyzing situations, offering solutions, demonstrating expertise—you're maintaining a particular identity that requires constant monitoring and adjustment. You're continually evaluating how well you're doing as the helpful person, the competent advisor, the solution provider.

This performance is exhausting because it never stops. Even in moments of supposed relaxation, part of your mind is scanning for problems to solve, opportunities to demonstrate value, and situations where your expertise might be needed.

Authentic presence, while initially uncomfortable because it requires dropping the performance, is ultimately less energy intensive. You don't have to maintain an identity or prove your worth. You can simply be with whatever is happening, without needing to fix, improve, or optimize it.

"I noticed something strange," Anders shared during a brief call we had. "After conversations where I was genuinely present without trying to solve anything, I felt energized rather than depleted. But after conversations where I was in consultant mode—even when I was supposedly 'helping'—I felt exhausted. Both mentally and physically."

This observation points to something fundamental about sustainable leadership and sustainable relationships: Presence generates the energy it requires, while performance depletes the energy it needs to maintain itself.

This distinction between presence and performance has become more pronounced as artificial intelligence enters our professional lives. AI is, in many ways, the perfect performance tool. It can analyze situations, generate solutions, and demonstrate expertise without fatigue. It never tires of being competent.

I've watched leaders respond to this capability in two very different ways.

Some use AI to become even more competent, more productive, more solution oriented. They delegate routine analysis to the machine and fill the recovered time with more complex problem-solving. Their professional performance becomes more sophisticated, but their capacity for presence doesn't change. The competence barrier becomes reinforced with better technology.

Others recognize something different: If AI can handle the performance work, perhaps they can finally make space for the presence work. If the machine can analyze the data and draft the strategic options, perhaps the human can be freed to do what only humans can do: Sit with uncertainty, offer genuine curiosity, be present without agenda.

Anders noticed this pattern in his own life. "I started using AI to prepare for client meetings," he told me. "It could synthesize the background, identify the key issues, even suggest approaches. And at first, I used that time to prepare even more sophisticated analyses. I was becoming a more impressive consultant."

He paused. "Then I realized I was using technology to build a higher competence barrier. More preparation, more expertise, more distance from actual human connection. The tools were making me better at performance and worse at presence."

The shift came when Anders started using the time differently. "Now I use AI for the analytical work, and I use the time it saves to prepare myself for presence. Not more information, but more capacity to listen, to be curious, to sit with whatever my client or my daughter needs from me."

AI cannot replicate *ro*. It cannot be calm and present in uncertainty. It can process and respond, but it cannot simply be with another person in their experience. This is not a limitation of current technology that future versions will solve. It's a fundamental difference between what machines do and what humans are.

The question for leaders like Anders isn't whether AI makes them more competent. It almost certainly does. The question is whether they use that competence to build higher walls or to create more space for genuine connection.

Cross-Cultural Perspectives on Presence and Connection

The tension between productivity and presence plays out differently depending on where you grew up and what your culture taught you about being valuable.

- **The American approach** treats presence as something to be earned through achievement. Time with loved ones becomes a reward for hard work rather than a practice. Many American executives I work with describe feeling "unproductive" when they're simply present with family, as if connection without accomplishment represents wasted time. The cultural message runs deep: Your worth is what you produce. Presence that doesn't generate measurable outcomes can feel like laziness disguised as love.

- **The Scandinavian approach** offers a different logic. Nordic cultures value *kvalitetstid* (quality time) and build social structures that protect space for family dinners, evening hours, and summer holidays. The assumption is that presence itself has value, not because it makes you more productive later, but because connection is the point. This doesn't mean Scandinavian leaders are automatically better at being present. Anders, after all, is Norwegian. But the cultural permission to prioritize presence without justifying it in terms of productivity creates different starting conditions.
- **The Asian approach** centers on relational harmony and role fulfillment. In many East Asian contexts, presence is expressed through duty, provision, and sacrifice rather than emotional availability in the Western sense. A Japanese executive once told me, "My father showed love by working himself to exhaustion for our family. He was rarely home, but his absence was his presence." This framing challenges Western assumptions about what connection requires, though it carries its own costs when children need emotional attunement rather than material security.
- **The British approach** tends toward understatement. Reserved presence, quality time expressed through shared activities rather than direct emotional conversation. "We don't talk about feelings," one London-based CEO told me. "We go fishing together. That's how we connect." The danger is mistaking physical proximity for genuine presence, but the strength is that connection doesn't always require verbal processing.

None of these approaches is wrong. Each reflects different cultural wisdom about how human beings connect. The question is whether your inherited approach is serving your relationships, or whether it's become another form of hiding.

The Scandinavian Concept of Samtale

There's another Norwegian word that became important in Anders's work: *samtale*. It translates as "conversation," but carries a more profound connotation—the kind of dialogue where both people are genuinely curious about each other's experience rather than waiting to share their own perspective or solutions.

Samtale requires what Scandinavians call *at være nærværende*—a quality of present attentiveness that makes the other person feel truly seen and heard. It's the opposite of the transactional conversations that dominate professional life, where everyone is positioning, persuading, or proving something.

Anders began experimenting with being laser focused on *samtale* in his relationships—with his daughter, his ex-wife, even his colleagues at the consulting firm. Instead of bringing solutions to conversations, he brought curiosity. Instead of demonstrating his expertise, he asked genuine questions about others' experiences.

"The first time I tried this with my ex-wife, she asked if I was feeling okay," Anders said, laughing. "She wasn't used to me being curious about her thinking without immediately offering my analysis. It took several conversations before she started to trust that I was genuinely interested rather than gathering information for some other purpose."

But gradually, something shifted. His ex-wife began sharing more honestly about her experience of co-parenting. His daughter started calling him not just when she needed help, but when she wanted connection. His colleagues at work began bringing him different kinds of challenges—not just the ones requiring solutions, but the ones requiring collaborative thinking, or even an empathetic ear.

The quality of his relationships was changing because the quality of his presence was changing.

What I Wish I'd Known: Presence as Leadership Development

If I could go back and tell my younger self one thing about leading as a Whole Human, it would be this: Presence isn't the opposite of competence—it's the foundation that makes competence sustainable.

When you show up authentically in relationships, you create psychological safety for others to do the same. When you can be uncertain and curious rather than always having answers, you build collaborative capacity rather than dependent teams. When you stop hiding in expertise, you model the vulnerability that makes a real connection possible.

The question isn't "How can I be more present?" but "What am I hiding from when I default to performance?" This shift from technique to self-awareness changes everything about how you approach both leadership and relationships.

The Ripple Effect of Authentic Presence

About six months into this work—though real change doesn't happen in neat timeframes—Anders shared stories that illuminated how presence work creates systemic change.

He was having dinner with his daughter and her boyfriend, the first time he'd met the young man. Anders felt his consultant mind activating, ready to evaluate this person's suitability, ask pointed questions, and demonstrate father-level competence.

Instead, he decided to practice presence. He asked simple, genuine questions about how they met, what they enjoyed doing together, and what the boyfriend was studying at university. When his daughter talked about a challenge with her thesis advisor, Anders didn't offer advice—he asked how she was thinking about handling it.

"About halfway through dinner, I realized I was enjoying myself," Anders told me. "I wasn't performing the role of protective father or demonstrating my wisdom. I was just present with these two young people, genuinely curious about their lives. And they opened in ways I don't think they would have if I'd been in consultant mode."

After the boyfriend left, Anders's daughter hugged him and said, "That was nice, Dad. He liked you. I liked you too."

"The way she said, 'I liked you too'—like she was rediscovering someone she'd lost," Anders reflected. "That's when I realized how much distance I had created."

A week later, his daughter asked him if he'd been in therapy. She'd noticed he was different—more present, less performative. She said it felt like talking to the father she remembered from childhood, before he became so important at work.

The changes extended beyond his family.

"I'm still good at my job," Anders reflected. "But I'm good at it differently now. Instead of always having the solution, I create space for others. Instead of managing everyone's emotions, I'm honest about my own uncertainty. The result is a team that trusts me more because they know I'm showing up authentically rather than performing expertise."

His ex-wife noticed too.

"She told me something interesting," Anders shared. "She said she used to feel like she was competing with my mind for my attention. Now she feels like we're working together on the complexities of raising a child. The difference isn't that I'm more available—my schedule hasn't changed dramatically. The difference is that when I'm present, I'm present."

This is perhaps the most critical insight about presence work: It's not about time management or work-life balance or productivity optimization. It's about developing the capacity to show up authentically in whatever context you're in, without hiding behind professional performance or protecting yourself with expertise.

Questions for Reflection

Transformational Question: "Who are you when you're not producing?"

This question cuts to the heart of the absent leader pattern. If your sense of worth is entirely tied to productivity, achievement, and professional competence, then any context that requires simply being present will feel threatening. But what if you could be valuable—to yourself and others—simply through the quality of your presence rather than the quantity of your production?

Consider this possibility: The relationships you've been avoiding might not need you to be more productive. They might need you to be more human. Becoming more human makes you a more effective leader, not despite your vulnerability but because of it.

Personal Awareness: "When do you feel most worthy—when you're achieving or when you're simply being present? What does this tell you?"

Notice how you answer this question. Many high achievers will intellectually know that presence matters, but emotionally feel most valuable when they're accomplishing, solving, or achieving something. This gap between what you know and what you feel reveals where the real work is.

Consider: Are there contexts where you feel safe being uncertain? Relationships where you don't need to have answers? Moments when you're valuable simply for being present rather than being productive? What would it mean to expand those contexts?

Systemic Thinking: "How does your professional culture make it difficult to be present? What would change if presence were valued as much as productivity?"

Look beyond individual behavior to organizational systems. Does your company reward people who respond to emails immediately, work long hours, and always have solutions? Are there implicit expectations that competence means certainty? What would change if your organization explicitly valued presence, curiosity, and collaborative problem-solving?

Action-Oriented: "What would change this week if you practiced being fully present in one relationship without trying to 'add value'?"

Choose one person—partner, child, friend, colleague—and experiment with presence without agenda. Just listen without offering solutions. Be curious without analyzing the witness without trying to fix. Notice what happens to the relationship, to your energy, to their responses.

Integration: "Beyond your professional identity, who are you? What aspects of yourself have you neglected while focusing on performance?"

This is often the most challenging question because we've become so identified with our professional roles that we've forgotten there are other ways to be valuable, other sources of meaning, different dimensions of our humanity. What did you love before you became successful at work? What parts of yourself feel dormant or neglected?

From Performance to Presence

The absent leader hides behind professional competence when personal relationships require vulnerable authenticity. But presence, unlike performance, is sustainable. Authentic relationships, unlike perfect ones, generate the energy they need rather than depleting it.

The hardest thing to learn is that showing up without answers isn't failure—it's the foundation of connection. And connection, it turns out, isn't just good for relationships. It's suitable for leadership.

But learning to be present without an agenda raises a deeper challenge: How do you lead in ways that develop others' capacity rather than reinforcing their dependence on your expertise? In Chapter 6, we'll explore the shift from solo genius to collaborative leadership—and why the most effective leaders aren't the ones with all the answers, but the ones who create conditions for collective intelligence to emerge.

6 Beyond Solo Genius

When collective intelligence surpasses individual brilliance.

I discovered the limits of solo genius while flat on my back with the flu, trapped in bed for three days in my East Dulwich house. Through the fever haze and the rain-streaked windows, I could hear the sounds of South London continuing to function without central command—the rhythmic thud of the 176 bus going past, conversations drifting up from the pavement, someone practicing piano three doors down with determined irregularity.

On the second day, curiosity got the better of my exhaustion. I dragged myself to the window overlooking the street. The pavement was slick with rain, reflecting the gray afternoon light, and what I saw below became one of those moments that shifts how you understand the world.

Two delivery drivers arrived at the same time, both needing to park in the single loading zone. Instead of competing for the space, they had a brief conversation through their windows. One backed up, let the other unload first, then took his turn. The whole interaction took two minutes and solved itself without conflict or oversight.

A teenager dropped her phone on the wet pavement. Before she could even react, an older man in a business suit had already bent to pick it up, checked that it wasn't cracked, and handed it back to her with a smile. She thanked him, he nodded, and both went on with their days, a tiny moment of care between strangers.

These patterns happen everywhere, but we just do not notice them. Pedestrians naturally make space for each other at narrow points. A woman with a pram was struggling with the café door, and someone inside was pushing it open for her before she even had to ask. Neighbors collect deliveries for each other. Shop owners helping tourists with directions. An entire ecosystem of mutual support operating without meetings, org charts, or anyone in charge.

I realized, lying there with used tissues scattered around me like evidence of my mortality, that I had spent years trying to be the indispensable center of every system I touched. At work, I insisted on being involved in every significant decision. In my projects, I held all the threads—timelines, resources, problem-solving, and quality control. I had confused being needed with being valuable.

But watching this ordinary South London street navigate the complexities of daily life without any central authority, I understood something I'd been missing: The highest form of leadership might not be making yourself indispensable, but creating conditions where others can flourish without you.

Janteloven: The Danish Case Against Solo Genius

That afternoon, as I drifted in and out of fevered sleep, I kept thinking about a Danish concept that suddenly made more sense than it ever had before: *janteloven*, literally "the law of Jante."

In American culture, *janteloven* is often misunderstood as a way of cutting down tall poppies, of discouraging excellence or individual achievement. But that's not quite right. What *janteloven* captures is the recognition that no one person is more important than the collective, not as a way to diminish individual brilliance, but as an understanding that sustainable success comes from collective capability rather than solo genius.

The solution isn't to be the most intelligent person in the room and solve every problem yourself. The solution is to create conditions where your team's collective intelligence surpasses what any individual—including you—could accomplish alone.

This flies in the face of everything American business culture celebrates. We worship the solo founder, the visionary CEO, the genius who sees what others miss. Our stories are about individuals who changed the world through force of will and brilliance of insight. The lone wolf who disrupts entire industries.

But here's what that mythology misses: Even those legendary individual leaders succeeded not because they did everything themselves, but because they created conditions where exceptional teams could do exceptional work. Steve Jobs didn't design and build every Apple product. Elon Musk doesn't personally engineer every Tesla. The magic happens in the space between visionary leadership and distributed execution.

Janteloven isn't about suppressing excellence. It's about recognizing that authentic leadership creates more leaders, not more followers.

The Control Addiction

I first recognized my own control addiction about six years ago, during a session with a leadership team in Paris. We were working on a strategy project, and I found myself increasingly frustrated that the team wasn't arriving at the conclusions I'd already reached in my preparation.

Instead of facilitating their thinking, I was steering them toward my answers. Instead of drawing out their insights, I was presenting my analysis. Instead of creating conditions for collective intelligence, I was performing solo genius.

During a break, one of the team members—a quietly brilliant operations director named Amélie—pulled me aside.

"You're not really asking us what we think," she said with the directness I've come to appreciate in French colleagues. "You're testing whether we can guess what you've already decided. If you already know the answer, just tell us. If you genuinely want our thinking, then actually listen to it."

She was right, and it stung. I had hired smart people, brought them together for their expertise, and then subtly communicated that their value was in validating my conclusions rather than generating their own insights.

This is what I call the control addiction—the pattern where leaders unconsciously undermine the very collaboration they claim to want because they can't let go of being the person with the answer.

Control addiction shows up in predictable ways:

- **Micromanagement disguised as quality control:** You review every detail not because it's necessary, but because you can't tolerate the anxiety of not knowing exactly what's happening.
- **Bottleneck leadership:** You insist on being involved in every decision, which slows everything down and prevents your team from developing its own judgment.
- **Expertise hoarding:** You keep critical knowledge and relationships centralized with yourself rather than developing those capabilities throughout your team.
- **Rescue patterns:** You step in to solve problems before your team has a chance to work through them, which feels helpful but actually prevents learning.
- **Quality perfectionism:** You set impossibly high standards that ensure only you can meet expectations, then use this as evidence that you need to maintain control.

The irony is brutal: The more you try to ensure quality through control, the more you prevent your team from developing the capability to deliver quality independently. You create the dependency you fear, then use that dependency to justify maintaining control.

Amélie's feedback struck me because I recognized my own pattern. But I'd also started seeing how this control addiction was evolving among the senior leaders I worked with.

David, a 58-year-old strategic consultant, came to me in crisis. For thirty years, he'd been one of the top analysts in his firm—the person who could look at a market and see patterns others missed. Then a 26-year-old analyst solved in forty-five minutes what would have taken David three days.

"I watched her work," he told me in Copenhagen. "She asked the AI questions. It gave her frameworks. She refined them. In less than an hour, she had something that would have taken me dozens of hours to develop."

"Was it good?" I asked.

"It was . . . adequate. Maybe 70% of what I would have done. But she'll get better. The tool will get better."

He paused. "And I'm sitting here wondering what I'm for."

This was the modern version of control addiction—holding onto expertise as your primary value when the world had shifted. David's superpower had been knowing things. Now everyone can learn things.

"What was wrong with her analysis?" I asked.

He thought about it. "It missed context, the political dynamics in that industry. The relationship between the CEO and board chair would shape any strategy. The fact that their last consultant promised transformation and delivered chaos, so they're skeptical of big changes."

"Could AI have told her that?"

"No. That's experience. Judgment. Knowing what matters beyond the data."

"That's what you're for," I said. "Not being the smartest person in the room anymore. Being the wisest. Teaching her to see what the analysis can't show."

David left relieved and terrified—relieved because he had a path forward, scared because it required letting go of being the hero with all the answers.

Breaking control addiction requires something uncomfortable: Acknowledging that your value as a leader isn't diminished when others succeed without you. In fact, it's amplified. The leader who develops other leaders creates an exponential impact that far exceeds what any individual contributor can achieve.

Cross-Cultural Approaches to Collective Intelligence

Working with teams across different cultures has taught me that distributed leadership isn't culturally neutral. Other societies have developed various approaches to balancing individual contribution with collective capability.

- **The American Approach—Individual Accountability Within Teams:** American business culture tends to emphasize individual accountability even within collaborative structures. Distributed leadership works best when it emphasizes personal ownership and clear performance metrics. The strength is entrepreneurial decision-making and rapid innovation. The limitation is that people may compete rather than truly collaborate, protecting their individual contributions rather than building on collective insights.

- **The German Approach—Systematic Delegation and Clear Authority:** German organizational culture values clear structures and systematic processes. Distributed leadership in this context means explicit delegation with well-defined authority boundaries. The strength is clarity and efficiency. The limitation can be rigidity and difficulty adapting when situations require flexibility beyond predefined roles.
- **The Danish Approach—Collective Responsibility and Flat Structures:** Scandinavian business culture, influenced by *janteloven*, naturally creates flatter hierarchies and more distributed decision-making. Teams expect to be involved in decisions that affect their work, and leadership is often more facilitative than directive. The strength is genuine collaboration and high trust. The limitation can be slower decision-making and difficulty when situations require decisive individual action.
- **The Japanese Approach—Consensus Through Process:** Japanese organizational culture emphasizes consensus-building and collective ownership through structured processes like *nemawashi* (building consensus before formal decisions). The strength is thorough consideration of perspectives and strong collective commitment once decisions are made. The limitation can be time intensity and difficulty with rapid pivots.

The key isn't choosing one cultural approach over another, but understanding how to adapt distributed leadership principles to fit your context while maintaining the core objective: developing collective capability that surpasses individual brilliance.

The Science Behind Collective Intelligence

The case for distributed leadership isn't a philosophical preference. Research consistently demonstrates that properly structured collective capability outperforms individual brilliance.

- **Team Intelligence Is Not the Sum of Member Intelligence.** MIT Center for Collective Intelligence research, conducted with Carnegie Mellon, studied 699 participants and found a general "c factor" (collective intelligence) that predicts team performance. Still, it is not correlated with average or maximum individual intelligence. What does predict collective intelligence: average social sensitivity, equality in conversational turn-taking, and proportion of females in the group. Capabilities emerge that transcend individual abilities.
- **Psychological Safety as Primary Driver.** Google's Project Aristotle studied 180 teams using 250 survey items and found the primary insight: "What really mattered was less about who is on the team, and more about how the team worked together." Psychological safety emerged as the number one factor. Teams with high psychological safety were rated as effective twice as often, with sales teams exceeding targets by 17% while low-safety teams fell short by up to 19%.
- **Shared Leadership Outperforms Hierarchy.** A meta-analysis of 42 independent samples found a strong positive relationship between shared leadership and team effectiveness. Effects were more potent when the work was more complex. A separate meta-analysis of 50 effect sizes from 3,198 teams confirmed that network-based shared leadership showed higher effect sizes than traditional approaches. Distributing leadership functions produces better results than relying on single hierarchical leaders.
- **The Curse of Knowledge.** Yale research demonstrated that expertise increases confidence in explanatory ability, but this confidence is unwarranted. Carnegie Mellon research found well-informed agents cannot accurately anticipate less-informed judgments, and the bias is difficult to correct. Expert leaders can become liabilities due to cognitive biases, supporting distributed decision-making where diverse perspectives that counterbalance blind spots.

Collective intelligence isn't about finding the most competent individuals. It's about creating conditions where groups think better together than any member could alone.

The Leadership Distribution Framework

After working with dozens of leadership teams struggling to let go of control, I developed a framework for thinking about which decisions to distribute and how. Not all decisions should be distributed, and distributed doesn't mean consensus on everything.

The framework has four categories:

- **Strategic Reserve** (10–15% of decisions): These are the decisions that truly require your unique perspective, authority, or accountability—setting overall direction, making high-stakes bets, managing board relationships, handling critical conflicts that can't be resolved at other levels. These should be rare. If more than 15% of your decisions fall into this category, you're probably hanging onto control rather than exercising necessary leadership.
- **Consultative Autonomy** (30–40% of decisions): These are decisions where team members have the authority to decide, but you want to be consulted before they act—major hiring decisions, significant vendor contracts, new product features, or changes to team structure. This isn't about maintaining control—it's about ensuring they have the benefit of your experience and perspective when navigating complex situations. The key is that your input is advisory, not directive. They're genuinely free to decide differently from what you recommend, and you need to be okay with that.
- **Informed Autonomy** (30–40% of decisions): Team members make these decisions independently and inform you after the fact—project timelines, client communication approaches, budget allocation within approved limits, or process improvements. You're in the loop for awareness and coordination, but you're not part of the decision process. This is where most of your team's day-to-day work should live. The goal is to catch issues early if needed, not to second-guess decisions that have already been made thoughtfully.
- **Full Autonomy** (20–30% of decisions): These decisions are entirely distributed—daily scheduling, routine client requests, standard operating procedures, or internal team coordination. Team members decide and act without needing to inform you at

all. They handle it, learn from it, and move forward. You trust their judgment and capability enough that you don't need visibility into every choice. This is where real empowerment lives.

The mistake most leaders make is keeping too many decisions in the Strategic Reserve and not enough in Full Autonomy. You end up as the bottleneck for everything, which slows the organization down and prevents your team from developing its capabilities.

I worked with a tech founder in Stockholm—let's call her Ingrid—who was struggling with this exact pattern. She prided herself on being accessible and involved, but her company had stalled at about sixty people because everything still flowed through her.

"I thought being available to help with every decision was good leadership," she told me during one of our sessions. "What I didn't realize is that I was training my team to be dependent rather than capable."

We mapped her decisions across these four categories. She was shocked to discover that over 60% of her decisions could have been made in Informed or Full Autonomy. Still, she'd been keeping them in Consultative or Strategic Reserve because she enjoyed being involved and trusted her own judgment more than her team's.

"The hard truth," she said, "is that I liked being needed. It made me feel valuable. What I missed is that the more they need me for decisions, the less they're developing their own capability. I was accidentally making myself indispensable, which felt good in the moment but was terrible for the company."

Over six months, we systematically redistributed her decisions. Some team members thrived immediately with more autonomy. Others needed development and coaching to build confidence in their decision-making. A few couldn't make the transition and moved on to roles where they were better suited.

But the company unstuck itself. Growth accelerated. Innovation increased because more people felt empowered to experiment. Ingrid found she had energy for actual strategic work rather than being buried in operational decisions.

"The weird part," she reflected, "is that I'm more valuable now than I was when I was essential to everything. My team trusts my strategic judgment more because I'm not second-guessing their operational decisions. I'm doing what only I can do rather than doing everything because I can."

Leader Spotlight: Letting Go

When I first met Mei Lin in Singapore, she was running a regional healthcare technology company with the kind of precision that makes investors comfortable. Every product decision flowed through her. Every client escalation landed on her desk. Her team of forty-something people described her as "kind but exhausting."

"I built this company from nothing," she told me during our first session, stirring tea in a café overlooking Marina Bay. "I know every system, every client relationship, every technical limitation," and then she added, "How can I trust someone else to care as much as I do?"

The turning point came when Mei Lin was hospitalized for two weeks with a kidney infection. For the first time in seven years, she had no choice but to let go.

"I expected disaster," she admitted later. "Instead, my product lead decided on a feature rollback that I would have agonized over for days. She just did it. And it was the right call."

What Mei Lin discovered during those two weeks changed how she understood her role. Her team hadn't been incapable. They'd been waiting for permission that never came.

We worked together on systematically redistributing decisions using the Leadership Distribution Framework. Mei Lin started with Informed Autonomy on product features, then expanded to Consultative Autonomy on client relationships. The hardest part, she said, wasn't trusting her team. It was tolerating the discomfort of not knowing everything.

Six months later, Mei Lin's company had expanded into two new markets. "I couldn't have done that while making every decision myself," she reflected. "The bottleneck wasn't my team's capability. It was my need to feel essential."

Her advice for other control-addicted leaders: "Start with one decision you're terrified to delegate. Then notice that the world doesn't end. That's your evidence that letting go creates more than it costs."

The Conditions for Collective Intelligence

Distributed leadership isn't just about pushing decisions down the org chart. It's about creating conditions where collective intelligence can emerge—where the team's thinking together produces insights that none of them could have generated individually.

This requires specific conditions that many organizations accidentally suppress:

- **Psychological Safety:** People need to be able to share half-formed ideas, challenge assumptions, admit uncertainty, and propose unconventional approaches without fear of judgment or punishment. When psychological safety is low, people default to safe thinking that reinforces the status quo. Collective intelligence requires cognitive risk-taking. Methods include starting meetings by sharing your own uncertainties first, explicitly thanking people for dissenting views, and separating idea generation from idea evaluation so early-stage thinking isn't immediately criticized.
- **Cognitive Diversity:** Teams composed of people who all think the same way don't generate collective intelligence—they generate groupthink. You need genuine diversity of perspective, experience, and thinking style. This includes but isn't limited to demographic diversity. The goal is to bring together people who naturally approach problems differently.
- **Structured Interaction:** Random group discussion doesn't produce collective intelligence. It requires facilitated processes that ensure all perspectives are heard, ideas are built upon systematically, and insights are captured and refined. Without structure, you get dominant voices drowning out others and good ideas getting lost in the chaos. Examples include round-robin input where everyone speaks before discussion begins, written pre-work so introverts can prepare their thinking, or designated devil's advocates who are expected to challenge emerging consensus.

- **Shared Mental Models:** While cognitive diversity is essential, team members need enough shared understanding of context, objectives, and constraints to have productive dialogue. Collective intelligence emerges at the intersection of diverse thinking and shared purpose. Create these through explicit alignment sessions on goals and constraints, visual frameworks that everyone references, and regular check-ins that surface differing assumptions before they derail progress.

When these conditions are present, something almost magical happens. Teams begin thinking together in ways that feel alive. Solutions emerge that surprise everyone, including the people creating them. Problems that seemed impossible become solvable through collective insight.

I saw this vividly with a product team in Copenhagen. They were stuck on a complex user experience challenge that had been debated for weeks without resolution. I facilitated a structured dialogue session where each person contributed their perspective on the problem without proposing solutions.

The engineering lead talked about technical constraints. The designer talked about user research insights. The product manager talked about business requirements. The customer support rep talked about actual user struggles she heard daily.

At first, these felt like competing priorities. But as the conversation continued and people genuinely listened to each other's perspectives, a solution emerged that none of them had thought of individually. It addressed all the constraints simultaneously by reframing the problem itself rather than trying to optimize within the existing problem definition.

"I've been on this team for two years," one engineer said afterward, "and that's the first time I felt like we actually thought together instead of just taking turns presenting our individual thoughts."

That's the difference between distributed work and collective intelligence. Distributed work is parallel processing—everyone doing their part independently. Collective intelligence is integrated thinking—the whole becoming genuinely greater than the sum of its parts.

What I Wish I'd Known: The Multiplier Effect

If I could go back and tell my younger self one thing about distributed leadership, it would be this: When you move from being the sole decision-maker to being the person who develops decision-makers, your impact multiplies exponentially.

One leader making 100 good decisions creates 100 units of value. One leader who enables 10 people to make 50 good decisions each creates 500 units of value. And those 10 people can develop others, creating geometric rather than arithmetic growth in organizational capability.

But the multiplication happens only when you genuinely let go of the need to be the most intelligent person in the room and embrace the challenge of creating room for others to be smart.

This shift requires something that feels counterintuitive: becoming more secure in your value by becoming less central to daily operations. Your worth as a leader isn't measured by how many problems you solve personally, but by how many problem-solvers you develop.

The Resistance You'll Face

Implementing distributed leadership inevitably encounters resistance—both from within yourself and from your organization. Understanding and preparing for this resistance is crucial for successful implementation.

Your Own Resistance

Your internal resistance to distributed leadership often manifests as the following:

- Fear that quality will decline without your direct oversight. This is sometimes valid, especially initially when team capability is still developing. But it becomes a self-fulfilling prophecy when you don't invest in building that capability.

- Anxiety about losing control over essential outcomes. Control feels like safety and giving it up feels dangerous. But the illusion of control through centralization often prevents you from seeing problems until they're too big to fix easily.
- Concern that your value will diminish if others make decisions. This reflects a fundamental misunderstanding of leadership value. Your value increases, not decreases, when you multiply capability rather than hoarding it.
- Worry that distributed decisions won't align with your vision. This is where the work of creating shared mental models becomes crucial. When people understand the why behind decisions, they can make aligned choices even when you're not involved.

Team Resistance

Your team's resistance to increased autonomy might include the following:

- Comfort with the current system, where you make difficult decisions. It's less risky for them when you own the outcomes. Taking responsibility is uncomfortable, especially if failure has historically been punished.
- Lack of confidence in their ability to make good decisions. This is often realistic—they may not yet have the judgment or context they need. This requires development, not just delegation.
- Preference for implementation roles rather than decision-making roles. Some people genuinely prefer executing well-defined plans to navigating ambiguity. That's okay—not everyone needs to be a decision-maker.
- Fear of increased accountability and visibility. When you make decisions that others can see and evaluate, you're more exposed to criticism. That vulnerability is real and requires cultural support to navigate.

Organizational Resistance

Organizational resistance to distributed leadership can manifest as the following:

- Performance management systems that reward individual contribution over capability development. If people are evaluated on what they personally accomplish rather than how they develop others, distributed leadership creates perverse incentives.
- Communication processes that assume hierarchical decision-making. When all essential communications flow through the leader, it reinforces centralization even when you're trying to distribute authority.
- Cultural norms that equate leadership visibility with leadership value. If leaders are expected to be in every meeting and make every decision, distributing leadership looks like abdication rather than development.
- Stakeholder expectations that you personally handle essential decisions. Board members, clients, or senior leadership may expect to interact with you directly rather than your empowered team. Resetting these expectations requires explicit conversation and demonstrated results.

The Decision Redistribution Audit

Before you can effectively distribute leadership, you need to understand your current decision patterns and identify opportunities for redistribution.

Week 1: Decision Tracking

For one whole week, track every significant decision that comes to you. Don't change your behavior—just observe and document:

- What was the decision?
- Who brought it to you?

- Why did it come to you rather than being decided elsewhere?
- How much time did it take?
- Could someone else have made this decision with the proper support?

Week 2: Pattern Analysis

Review your decision log and categorize each decision using the Leadership Distribution Framework:

- How many fell into the Strategic Reserve? (Should be 10–15%)
- How many were Consultative Autonomy? (30–40%)
- How many were Informed Autonomy? (30–40%)
- How many were Full Autonomy? (20–30%)

Look for patterns:

- Which types of decisions are you holding onto unnecessarily?
- Where are you a bottleneck?
- What decisions could be distributed with relatively little risk?
- What decisions require capability development before they can be distributed?

Week 3: Redistribution Experiment

Choose 3–5 decisions from your analysis that could be redistributed. For each one:

1. **Identify who** should make this decision going forward.
2. **Provide context:** Help them understand the why behind good choices in this domain.
3. **Set boundaries:** Clarify what constraints or principles should guide their choice.
4. **Establish feedback loops:** How will you both learn from the outcomes?
5. **Commit to non-interference:** Resist the urge to swoop in unless truly necessary.

Week 4: Reflection and Adjustment

After your redistribution experiment:

- What went well? What was harder than expected?
- How did team members respond to increased autonomy?
- What capability gaps became visible?
- What adjustments do you need to make to your approach?
- What will you redistribute next?

This audit reveals where you're maintaining control out of habit rather than necessity and creates a systematic path toward more distributed leadership.

Questions for Reflection

Transformational Question: "What masterpiece could your team create if you let go?"

This question isn't rhetorical. It's an invitation to reimagine what becomes possible when you move beyond solo genius to collective intelligence.

Most leaders underestimate their team's potential because they've never created conditions for that potential to be fully expressed. When you distribute leadership effectively, you often discover capabilities in your team members that surprise both you and them.

The masterpiece your team could create isn't just better outcomes or more efficient processes. It's a way of working together that generates continuous innovation, adapts rapidly to change, and develops leadership capability at every level of the organization.

It's an organization that can scale beyond your individual capacity, survive your absence, and ultimately exceed what you could have built through solo leadership, no matter how brilliant your personal contributions.

But accessing this potential requires letting go of the familiar comfort of control and trusting the uncertain adventure of collective capability. It requires believing that the collective intelligence of your empowered team can surpass your individual intelligence, no matter how capable you are.

The masterpiece exists in the space between your vision and their capability, between your strategic thinking and their diverse perspectives, between your experience and their fresh insights.

What could that masterpiece look like in your context?

Personal Awareness: "Where do you default to doing things yourself rather than trusting others? What are you afraid would happen if you truly let go?"

Notice where the fear lives. Is it really about quality, or is it about needing to feel essential? Are you protecting the organization from potential failure, or protecting yourself from the discomfort of not being in control? Sometimes our most persistent control patterns are the ones protecting our identity rather than our outcomes.

Systemic Thinking: "How does your organization reward individual heroics versus collective success? What would change if collaboration were the primary measure?"

Look honestly at your formal and informal reward systems. Do people get promoted because they personally achieved something impressive, or because they developed others' capabilities? Are heroes celebrated more than team players? Do performance reviews focus on individual contribution or collective impact? Systems shape behavior more than intentions do.

Action-Oriented: "What would you delegate or share this week that you've been holding onto? How will you create space for others to contribute?"

Start small, but start now. Choose one decision you've been making that someone else could make with the proper context and support. Give them that context. Set clear boundaries. Then practice the most challenging part of distributed leadership: staying out of the way unless they specifically ask for input.

Integration: "Where else in your life do you over-function? How might shared responsibility strengthen your relationships?"

The patterns that show up in your leadership usually show up in your personal relationships, too. Do you struggle to let your partner handle things differently from you would? Do you take over projects rather than letting your kids work through challenges? Do you organize everything for your friends rather than creating space for shared ownership? Distributed leadership isn't just a professional skill—it's a human capacity that transforms all your relationships.

The Masterpiece You Can't Build Alone

Solo genius is seductive because it's familiar. You know what you can do. Collective intelligence is uncertain because it requires trusting what others might do. But organizations that scale, adapt, and sustain themselves over time are never built on the genius of one person. They're built on systems that develop genius in many.

The question isn't whether you can let go. The question is whether you're willing to discover what becomes possible when you do.

But distributed leadership only works when people can hear each other—when brutal truths can be spoken and hard conversations can be had without destroying relationships or derailing progress. In Chapter 7, we'll explore what it takes to create cultures where truth-telling is safe and necessary conversations happen.

7 From Burnout to Breakthrough

The systematic approach to recovery and redesign.

The refrigerator hums. The coffee maker sits ready on the counter, still warm from her partner's morning routine an hour ago. Through the kitchen window of her Östermalm apartment, Stockholm is already moving: cyclists heading toward Strandvägen, the morning ferry crossing toward Djurgården. March is getting underway, and the month feels both crisp and gray at once.

Elena has been standing in front of the open refrigerator for too long.

Eggs or yogurt. Toast or granola. Coffee or tea. The questions loop in her mind without resolution. Her teenage daughter left for school without saying goodbye—again. Her partner kissed her forehead on his way out, that gentle gesture that's become a worried check-in. The board presentation she's supposed to deliver in three hours sits unfinished on her laptop in the other room.

She closes the refrigerator without taking anything.

Opens it again.

Her hands are shaking slightly. This is ridiculous. She has a PhD in biochemistry from Karolinska Institute. She's led three successful drug approval processes. She manages a 400-person organization with a budget of €175 million. And she cannot decide what to eat for breakfast.

The realization arrives with sudden, terrible clarity: Something is very wrong.

She leaves the kitchen, walks past her home office where regulatory documents she couldn't process at midnight are still glowing on two monitors, and sits on the edge of her bed. Her phone shows seventeen unread messages, three from her VP of operations about the restructuring plan. Two board members are asking for updates, five from her team about yesterday's crisis meeting. The rest are automated alerts from systems that never sleep.

She picks up her phone. Scrolls through her contacts. Finds the number for the speaker she met at a conference last year—the Danish guy who'd talked about sustainable leadership in a way that seemed almost subversive in a room full of high achievers.

What was his name? Peter something.

She types: "I think I need help."

Deletes it.

Types: "Is this what burnout feels like?"

Deletes it.

Finally, types: "Can we talk?" and hits send before she can overthink it.

Three weeks later, I'm walking with Elena along the Charlottenlund forest loop north of Copenhagen. It's the same path I walked, what feels like 847 times in the months after my own breakdown—oak and birch trees creating a natural cathedral overhead, the sound of gravel crunching under our feet, the ocean smell carried inland on the wind.

Elena is on day twenty-one of what we're calling her stabilization phase. She's taken a one-month protected leave—a decision that felt terrifying but necessary. Her days now follow a structure so simple it seemed almost insulting when her psychologist first prescribed it: sleep, eat, move, connect. Nothing else.

"I keep thinking I should be doing more," she says, adjusting her pace to match mine. "I have a list in my head of hundreds of things I need to fix when I get back. The restructuring plan. The VP situation. The three drug approval processes are behind schedule. The relationship with my daughter is basically nonexistent. My partner, who's exhausted from holding everything together."

We walk in silence for a moment. A jogger passes going the opposite direction, earbuds in, lost in their own rhythm.

"What did you eat for breakfast this morning?" I ask.

She smiles slightly. "Yogurt with granola. And coffee. It only took me three minutes to decide."

"Three weeks ago?"

"Twenty minutes. Standing in front of an open refrigerator, as if it contained the mysteries of the universe instead of just dairy products and vegetables."

This is where we start, not with the big problems: the board pressure, the pipeline delays, the toxic leadership dynamics, the family strain. We begin with breakfast decisions. With nervous system regulation. We need to build back the basic capacity to function before we try to rebuild the complex capacity to lead.

When Everything Stops Working

Elena's situation was what I call complexity burnout—not too much of one thing, but too many impossible things happening simultaneously.

Her pharmaceutical company was navigating final-stage approvals for three separate drugs, each representing years of research and hundreds of millions in investment. The board was pressing for a 12% headcount reduction while simultaneously demanding faster product launches. Her VP of operations had deep relationships with key board members but was creating a toxic environment that had driven away two promising directors in the past year. Regulatory agencies were asking questions that required technical depth she no longer had the cognitive capacity to provide.

And at home, her teenage daughter had stopped talking to her beyond monosyllables. Her partner was handling everything from school pickups to dinner to homework help—essentially functioning as a single parent while Elena worked seventy-hour weeks.

"The worst part," Elena tells me during one of our early sessions, "is that I know I should be able to handle this. I've managed larger teams, bigger budgets, and more complex problems. I learned during my MBA at Harvard that great leaders push through. My first job in Boston at a US pharma company taught me that the people who succeed are the ones who work the hardest. So why do I feel like I'm drowning in shallow water?"

This is the cultural collision that makes Elena's burnout particularly complex. She's Swedish by birth and upbringing, but she spent six formative years absorbing American achievement culture—first at Harvard Business School, then in her late twenties and early thirties at a Boston-based pharmaceutical company. She learned to lead the American way: faster, harder, longer, more.

Then she returned to Sweden to join one of the country's largest pharmaceutical companies, bringing American intensity to a Scandinavian context. The result was internal conflict that compounded her exhaustion. Not pushing hard enough by American standards. Too intense by Swedish cultural norms. Failing both systems simultaneously.

What Elena was experiencing—what I had experienced, what thousands of leaders experience—isn't weakness. It's the predictable outcome of operating beyond sustainable capacity for too long, especially when you're trying to meet incompatible cultural expectations.

This is the paradox of high-achievement burnout. You can be successful by every external measure while feeling empty inside. The very systems that create external success often systematically deplete internal resources.

The European Perspective on Recovery

In Nordic cultures, we have a concept called *eftertænksomhed*—being thoughtful and reflective. It's the practice of deliberately pausing to consider not just what to do next, but what the situation requires, what you're capable of providing, and whether the two align.

Eftertænksomhed stands in stark contrast to the American leadership culture that Elena, despite being Swedish, had internalized during her MBA in Boston and her early career at a US-based pharma company. American leadership culture emphasizes speed, decisiveness, and pushing through. If you're not growing, you're dying. If you're not optimizing, you're falling behind. If you're experiencing burnout, the solution is better time management, more efficiency, and stronger discipline.

But burnout isn't a failure of willpower. It's a failure of design. And you can't solve a design problem with willpower solutions.

The European approach to burnout recovery differs fundamentally from American models. In the US, recovery is often framed as individual resilience training—teaching people to bounce back faster, to be grittier, to develop stronger coping mechanisms. The underlying message: The system is fine; you just need to get tougher.

European workplace cultures, particularly in Scandinavia, treat burnout as a structural issue requiring systemic intervention. When someone burns out in Denmark or Sweden, the first question isn't "What's wrong with this person?" but "What's wrong with this situation?" Recovery involves not just individual healing but organizational redesign.

This cultural difference shows up in everything from sick leave policies to leadership expectations. A Swedish leader taking two months of protected recovery time is supported and expected. An American leader taking the same time often faces potential career consequences.

Elena had been operating under American expectations in a Swedish context, creating internal conflict that compounded her burnout. "I felt like I was failing both systems," she explains. "Not pushing hard enough for my American board members, too intense for my Swedish team."

What I Wish I'd Known: The Recovery Paradox

Real recovery requires doing less, not more. It requires designing for sustainability, not just achievement. It requires treating your breakdown as valuable information rather than personal failure. And increasingly, it requires understanding what parts of leadership can be supported by technology—and what parts become more critical precisely because technology cannot do them.

The Co-Intelligence Question

Recovery from burnout now requires addressing a question previous generations of leaders didn't face: What parts of my leadership can be enhanced by artificial intelligence, and what parts become more critical precisely because AI cannot do them?

Elena's crisis revealed this dimension clearly. During our second conversation, she described her typical day: responding to 100+ emails (*How is that even possible?* I thought), attending eight meetings, making dozens of small decisions, reviewing reports, approving requests, and managing crises. "I feel like a costly information processing system," she said. "And not even a perfect one anymore."

This realization is becoming common among leaders facing burnout. They discover they've been burning out on tasks that AI could handle better, while neglecting the uniquely human capacities that matter.

One executive recovering from burnout told me: "I realized I was spending 60% of my time on things a sophisticated algorithm could do better, while the 40% that required my human judgment—building trust, reading complex emotional dynamics, making ethically nuanced decisions—was getting squeezed into the margins."

The European perspective on AI and recovery differs notably from the American approach. In the United States, AI is often positioned as a productivity accelerator—do more, faster, better. The implicit message: If AI makes you more efficient, you should use that efficiency to do even more.

In Scandinavian contexts, AI is increasingly framed as a tool to reclaim human capacity for what humans do best: creative thinking, ethical reasoning, relationship building, and making decisions with incomplete information in complex social contexts.

This isn't about AI replacing leaders. It's about AI handling the cognitive overhead that was never what leadership was truly about in the first place. The leaders who recover most effectively from burnout are those who learn to use AI not as a crutch for doing more, but as a tool for redesigning their role around their irreplaceable human capacities.

For Elena, this meant beginning to distinguish between three types of decisions:

- **Routine decisions that AI could handle:** Scheduling, routine approvals, information synthesis, pattern recognition in data, drafting standard communications.
- **Decisions requiring human judgment with AI support:** Strategic choices where AI could provide analysis, but humans

must weigh competing values, decisions involving ethical complexity, and situations requiring cultural or emotional nuance.

- **Decisions requiring purely human capacity:** Building trust across the organization, reading political dynamics on the board, knowing when someone needs support versus challenge, and making calls with incomplete information in ambiguous situations.

"I thought I was irreplaceable because I worked harder than anyone else," Elena reflects months later. "I'm actually irreplaceable because of capacities that have nothing to do with processing speed or working hours—and everything to do with being human."

The Science Behind Recovery

Recovery from burnout isn't wishful thinking. Research provides evidence-based protocols and measurable markers for systematic rebuilding.

- **Recovery Is Possible at Scale.** Mayo Clinic and Stanford data showed burnout dropping from 62.8% in 2021 to 45.2% in 2023, a 17-point improvement when organizational and individual interventions were implemented. The researchers note: "With chronic stress exposure, prefrontal gray matter connections are lost, but they can be restored by stress relief." The damage is real, but reversible.
- **Objective Recovery Biomarkers.** Institute of Stress Medicine research in Gothenburg, Sweden, compared patients with clinical burnout against controls and found that all heart rate variability measures were significantly lower in burnout patients. Low HRV reflects low parasympathetic activity and, accordingly, low regenerative capacity. This provides objective metrics for tracking nervous system recovery, making the invisible visible.
- **Exercise as Evidence-Based Intervention.** A systematic review of longitudinal and intervention studies found strong evidence for physical activity reducing exhaustion. The cardiovascular fitness hypothesis explains that regular physical activity enables better

handling of psychological stress and faster bodily recovery after exposure. Exercise is proven medicine for burnout with robust effect sizes.

- **Return-to-Work Success Factors.** Swedish research on return-to-work interventions found that 89% returned to work at 18-month follow-up with a workplace-oriented intervention focused on job-person fit through patient-supervisor communication. Combined person-directed and organization-directed approaches proved superior to single-level interventions. Sustainable reintegration requires both individual recovery and organizational redesign.
- **Long-Term Outcomes.** The LANE Study at Karolinska Institute followed 2,474 nurses for 11–15 years and found that outcomes were significantly affected by earlier burnout, including turnover, absenteeism, and cardiovascular problems. However, research also found early career burnout, when addressed, led to greater flexibility in work approach. A crisis can catalyze positive redesign when properly supported.

Recovery requires systematic intervention, not just rest, addressing individual, relational, and organizational factors simultaneously.

The Recovery Roadmap: A Systematic Approach

Recovery from burnout follows predictable patterns, just as the decline into burnout does. Understanding these patterns allows us to create a systematic approach rather than hoping recovery will just happen naturally.

The Recovery Roadmap consists of four interconnected phases, each building on the previous one. Unlike traditional recovery models that focus primarily on rest and restoration, this approach treats recovery as active rebuilding—creating something better than what existed before.

Phase 1: Stabilization (Weeks 1–6)

Foundation: "I am learning to be steady again."

The priority isn't productivity—it's stability. Your nervous system has been in chronic activation mode. Before you can build anything new, you need to create safety and predictability.

For me, this phase began with four simple instructions from my psychologist, written in Danish and taped to my wall: sleep, eat, spend time with Theo, and exercise. Nothing else.

During stabilization, Elena used what she called her "AI triage system"—a way to reduce her cognitive load while she rebuilt her capacity.

Each morning, an AI assistant sorted her incoming requests into three categories:

- **Immediate personal attention:** Strategic decisions, sensitive personnel matters, board communications—approximately 15% of incoming demands.
- **Delegated with AI-generated context:** Operational choices with clear parameters, where her team could decide with proper background information—approximately 50% of demands.
- **AI-handled with human oversight:** Routine approvals, scheduling, information synthesis, standard communications—approximately 35% of demands.

This simple system reduced Elena's daily decision load significantly, freeing mental energy for recovery. More importantly, it revealed how much of her burnout came from treating every decision as equally important.

Core stabilization practices include the following:

- **Sleep Structures:** Establishing consistent sleep and wake times, regardless of how much work feels urgent. Elena began with a strict 10 p.m. to 6 a.m. sleep schedule, treating it as non-negotiable as a board meeting.
- **Energy Mapping:** Tracking what activities give energy versus what drains it. Elena discovered that her one-on-ones with direct reports energized her, while group meetings with her VP of operations depleted her for hours afterward. (See Chapter 4 for details on energy mapping.)

- **Boundary Setting:** Creating clear start and stop times for work. Elena implemented a hard stop at 5:30 p.m., giving her evening time with her daughter and partner. The first week was torture, she admits during one of our walks. By week three, she was shocked at how much more effective she was during working hours.
- **Nervous System Regulation:** Daily practices that activate your parasympathetic nervous system. For Elena, this meant thirty-minute walks in Stockholm's Djurgården park before work. For me, it was the Charlottenlund forest loop—seven kilometers through oak and birch trees that became my daily meditation.
- **The Scandinavian Design Principle:** Start with function, not form. Your job isn't to look recovered—it's to build the foundational systems that make recovery possible.

During this phase, both Elena and I struggled with what she called "recovery guilt"—the feeling that taking time to stabilize was selfish or lazy. This is common among high achievers who have learned to equate their worth with their productivity.

"I feel like I'm letting everyone down," Elena told me during week two.

"Who specifically are you letting down by creating the stability you need to be effective long-term?" I asked.

The question revealed the extent to which she had internalized unsustainable expectations. She wasn't letting anyone down—she was catching herself before she let everyone down through complete collapse.

Phase 2: Assessment (Weeks 7–12)

Foundation: "I am learning to see clearly again."

Once you've established basic stability, you can begin to assess what happened. This isn't about blame or shame—it's about understanding the systematic factors that led to burnout so you can design around them going forward.

Over coffee one afternoon in week five, she described what happened during her assessment phase. She'd worked with an AI system to audit her decision log over three months, identifying patterns she hadn't noticed: 73% of her "urgent" decisions were routine matters made urgent by lack of clear delegation frameworks. The truly strategic decisions requiring her expertise made up less than 15% of her time.

AI didn't tell her what to do—it showed her patterns she was too close to see herself. The challenge for recovering leaders in an AI-augmented world is distinguishing between decisions that genuinely require human judgment and those we're holding onto out of habit or control.

Core Assessment Practices included the following:

- **The Burnout Drivers Framework:** Identifying the specific factors that led to your burnout across four domains:
  - *Workload Drivers*: Volume of work, pace of work, complexity of challenges, decision density, and availability demands. For Elena, the combination of regulatory deadlines, board pressure, and toxic VP management created an impossible situation.
  - *Control Drivers*: Autonomy over how you work, ability to say no, decision-making authority, and schedule control. Elena had responsibility without absolute authority—accountable for outcomes she couldn't fully control.
  - *Values Drivers*: Alignment between your values and your work, ethical conflicts, meaning and purpose, identity integration. Elena realized she'd spent three years implementing layoffs that violated her core beliefs about developing people.
  - *Support Drivers*: Quality of relationships, team functionality, leadership support, resources available. Her toxic VP had poisoned team dynamics while her board provided pressure without support.
- **Energy Archaeology:** Looking back at when you felt most alive and effective in your leadership. Elena traced her energy patterns over five years, discovering she was most effective and energized when solving complex scientific problems, not managing political dynamics.
- **The Costs Audit:** Honestly assessing what burnout has cost you: relationships, health, opportunities, sense of self. Elena's daughter had stopped sharing anything meaningful with her. Her partner was exhausted. She hadn't seen her friends in months. The achievement she was so proud of had come at a price she wasn't willing to continue paying.

Cultural Perspective—Japanese Approach: In Japan, the concept of *karoshi* (death from overwork) is taken seriously enough to mandate legal protections. Japanese recovery approaches emphasize gradual reintegration and collective responsibility—the organization must change, not just the individual. Face-saving measures allow leaders to recover without professional stigma.

This perspective would become particularly relevant for Sofia's story, which I'll share later in this chapter.

Phase 3: Redesign (Weeks 13–20)

Foundation: "I am rebuilding differently."

With stability established and a clear understanding of what led to burnout, you can begin systematic redesign. This isn't about returning to how things were—it's about building something better.

Elena's redesign focused on three dimensions: work architecture, decision protocols, and human-AI collaboration.

Work Architecture Redesign Elena renegotiated her role with her board. She would focus on scientific strategy and key regulatory relationships—work that leveraged her PhD in biochemistry and her talent for complex problem-solving. The toxic VP's responsibilities were restructured, removing his direct reports from his management and placing them under Elena with more transparent accountability.

She built her "leadership council"—five trusted people across functions who met weekly to handle the operational decisions that had been consuming her time. This wasn't delegation without support—she created clear frameworks, decision rights, and escalation paths.

Decision Protection Through AI As Elena rebuilt her leadership approach, she made conscious choices about where AI fit in her redesigned systems. AI handled information gathering, pattern recognition in research data, regulatory document drafting, and routine communication templates. She focused on interpretation, relationship building, strategic direction, and the human judgment calls that no algorithm could make.

The question wasn't "What can AI do?" but "What am I uniquely positioned to contribute that AI cannot?" This distinction became foundational to her sustainable leadership model.

She implemented my Decision Protection Protocol (which I covered in detail in Chapter 4), batching similar decisions into specific time blocks, delegating routine choices to her leadership council, eliminating non-decisions that were draining her energy, and protecting morning hours for strategic thinking. The framework that had also helped Klaus and Marcus manage cognitive load now gave Elena the mental capacity she needed for recovery.

Human Capacity Reclamation Elena began scheduling "human work"—the activities that required uniquely human capabilities. Tuesday afternoons became one-on-one time with her direct reports. Wednesday mornings were reserved for walking meetings with her most creative scientists, where breakthrough thinking often happened. Friday afternoons were dedicated to building relationships with regulatory officials—work that required trust, nuance, and cultural understanding that no AI could replicate.

"I stopped trying to be a human algorithm and started being a human leader," she reflects during one of our monthly check-ins, six months into her recovery. "The irony is I'm far more effective now, working fewer hours, because I'm doing the work only I can do."

Cultural Perspective—Scandinavian Approach: Swedish workplace culture emphasizes collective responsibility and structural solutions. When Elena's company implemented her redesign, they didn't treat it as "Elena's accommodation" but as a pilot for better leadership design across the organization. Three other executives adopted similar approaches within the following year.

Phase 4: Integration (Weeks 21+)

Foundation: "This is how I lead now."

The final phase isn't about reaching a destination—it's about integrating recovery practices into ongoing leadership. What worked during the crisis becomes how you operate all the time.

For Elena, integration meant building sustainability practices into her regular rhythms:

- **Monthly Energy Audits:** Reviewing her calendar, decision log, and energy levels to identify drift back toward unsustainable patterns. She used a simple AI tool to track meeting density, decision load, and time allocation across her three core areas.
- **Quarterly Leadership Design Reviews:** Assessing whether her work architecture still aligned with her strengths and energy. Work demands change—leadership design must evolve with them.
- **Protected Practices:** The non-negotiables that keep her grounded. Morning walks in Djurgården. Evening time with her daughter. Weekly leadership council meetings. Fortnightly dinners with her partner without discussing work.
- **Continuous Learning:** Reading about burnout prevention, attending workshops on sustainable leadership, and learning from others' experiences. Recovery isn't a one-time event—it's an ongoing practice.

For me, integration looked different but followed the same principle. The Charlottenlund forest walks continued long after I was "recovered"—300+ walks in that first year, then hundreds more in the years since. They're no longer emergency therapy. They're how I think, how I process, how I stay connected to something larger than my work.

The ocean swimming I began that cold May morning became a year-round practice—a willingness to enter discomfort intentionally, knowing that what doesn't overwhelm you can strengthen you.

Leader Spotlight: Recovery Through Redefinition

Sofia started her AI company in San Francisco in 2019, building consumer tools that helped people manage information overload. The irony wasn't lost on her when she collapsed from information overload herself in early 2022.

"I was attempting to process information at machine speed, make decisions with algorithmic precision, and maintain superhuman availability," she reflects. "I was literally trying to out-AI the AI we were building."

Sofia's background made her situation particularly complex. Her father was Japanese, her mother American, and she'd spent her childhood moving between Tokyo and California. She'd absorbed both cultures' relationship with work—Japanese dedication and American hustle—creating internal expectations that were doubly impossible to sustain.

Her breakdown came during a product launch where she'd worked 127 hours in a single week, personally verifying every detail of the launch campaign, every customer service response, every piece of marketing copy. "I collapsed during the celebration party," she remembers. "Not dramatically—I just couldn't form coherent sentences anymore. My brain had simply stopped."

The months that followed required Sofia to confront a fundamental question: If AI can handle information processing, pattern recognition, and routine decision-making better than humans, what's left for human leaders to do?

The answer emerged gradually through her recovery process—everything AI cannot do.

Building trust across cultural boundaries and reading emotional undercurrents in team dynamics, making ethically complex decisions with incomplete information, holding space for creativity and experimentation, maintaining psychological safety, and knowing when to push and when to protect. These uniquely human capacities had atrophied while she'd been trying to be a human algorithm.

Sofia's Japanese heritage influenced her recovery approach in meaningful ways. In Japanese culture, the concept of *gradual reintegration* allows someone recovering from burnout to return to work incrementally, with face-saving measures that prevent professional stigma. Rather than announcing a "comeback," Sofia quietly reduced her hours, restructured her role, and rebuilt her capacity over six months.

"The turning point came when I started using AI as my research assistant and information processor, which freed up my cognitive capacity for what I'm good at," Sofia explains. "Understanding what my people need.

Building relationships with our enterprise clients. Making the judgment calls that require human intuition and ethical reasoning. Reading the subtle dynamics in investor meetings. Knowing when someone on my team is struggling before they say anything."

Her redesigned leadership model positions AI as infrastructure—handling information flow, pattern recognition, and routine operations—while she focuses on strategy, culture, relationships, and the complex human dynamics that determine whether technical capabilities translate into organizational success.

The transformation showed up in measurable ways. Employee satisfaction increased by 43%. Customer retention improved. Sofia's team reported feeling more supported and autonomous. Investors commented that her strategic thinking had sharpened rather than declined.

"I thought I was irreplaceable because I worked harder than anyone else," Sofia reflects. "I'm irreplaceable because of capacities that have nothing to do with processing speed or working hours—and everything to do with being human. That realization saved my company. But more importantly, it saved me."

Four months into her recovery, Sofia implemented a company-wide policy: no emails after 6 p.m., no weekend work unless truly critical, and mandatory vacation time. "We build AI tools that help people manage information overload," she explains. "It would be hypocritical if we burned ourselves out while doing it."

The Recovery Self-Assessment

Understanding which phase of recovery you're in helps you focus your energy appropriately. Rate yourself honestly across four domains on a scale of 1–10 (1 = severe difficulty, 10 = functioning well).

Physical Domain:

- Sleep quality and consistency: ___
- Energy levels throughout the day: ___
- Physical symptoms (tension, illness, pain): ___
- Exercise or movement practice: ___

Mental Domain:

- Ability to focus and concentrate: ___
- Decision-making confidence: ___
- Mental clarity: ___
- Cognitive endurance: ___

Emotional Domain:

- Emotional stability: ___
- Ability to feel positive emotions: ___
- Recovery from setbacks: ___
- Sense of hope or optimism: ___

Relational Domain:

- Quality of key relationships: ___
- Ability to be present with others: ___
- Communication effectiveness: ___
- Feeling connected versus isolated: ___

Scoring Guide (sum of points in each domain):

- *32–40 points (Stabilization Phase)*: Focus on basic recovery—sleep structures, nutrition, movement, and connection. Use AI to offload routine decisions. Protect your cognitive resources.
- *24–31 points (Assessment Phase)*: You have enough stability to begin understanding what led to burnout. Map your burnout drivers, audit your energy, and assess costs. Use AI tools to identify patterns you can't see yourself.
- *16–23 points (Redesign Phase)*: Time for systematic rebuilding. Renegotiate your role, create decision protocols, and implement human-AI collaboration frameworks. Build new structures for sustainable leadership.
- *Below 16 points (Crisis Mode)*: Seek professional support immediately. Consider medical evaluation, therapy, and potentially extended leave. This assessment suggests you need more intensive intervention than self-guided recovery.

For Any Score: If you're experiencing thoughts of self-harm, overwhelming despair, or complete inability to function, please contact a mental health professional immediately. Recovery is possible, but some situations require professional support.

The Science Behind Systematic Approaches

Recovery research consistently shows that systematic approaches are more effective than intuitive ones. This isn't because intuition is wrong, but because burnout impairs the very faculties, we need for good intuitive decision-making.

- **Cognitive Load Theory** explains why systems matter more than willpower. When you're recovering from burnout, your cognitive resources are already depleted. Having clear frameworks and systems reduces the mental energy required to make good choices, allowing your energy to go toward healing and growth rather than constant decision-making.
- Research from the Max Planck Institute for Human Cognitive and Brain Sciences demonstrates that **recovery from burnout** involves measurable neurological changes—rebuilding prefrontal cortex function that was impaired by chronic stress. This process takes time and requires cognitive rest, not just physical rest.
- **Implementation Intention Research** from NYU shows that people who create specific "if-then" plans are 3× more likely to follow through on desired changes. The Recovery Roadmap leverages this by providing concrete practices linked to specific phases and conditions.
- **Chronobiological Research** from the Oxford Sleep and Circadian Neuroscience Institute confirms that consistent sleep structures—not just more sleep—are critical for recovery. The brain's glymphatic system, which clears metabolic waste, functions primarily during quality sleep. Burnout disrupts this system; recovery requires rebuilding it.
- **Longitudinal Recovery Studies** from Karolinska Institute in Sweden tracked leaders recovering from burnout over two years. Those who followed systematic recovery approaches showed not just restoration but enhancement—better decision-making, stronger

emotional intelligence, and more sustainable performance patterns than before burnout.

- **AI and Cognitive Load Research:** Recent studies from MIT's Center for Collective Intelligence demonstrate that well-designed AI assistance can reduce routine decision fatigue by up to 40% without compromising decision quality. However, the research also shows a critical threshold. When AI systems make recommendations rather than simply processing information, humans often defer to AI judgment even when their own expertise would suggest a different course. The key to recovering leaders is using AI for information processing while maintaining human agency in actual decision-making.
- **Social Cognitive Theory** demonstrates that sustainable change happens through a combination of personal agency, environmental design, and behavioral modeling. The Recovery Roadmap addresses all three: It builds your sense of control, helps you redesign your environment, and provides examples of others who have successfully navigated similar transformations.
- Perhaps most importantly, **Post-Traumatic Growth Research** shows that people who experience and recover from significant challenges often develop capabilities they didn't have before. The systematic approach ensures that your recovery becomes not just healing, but genuine growth.

The Larger Context: What Recovery Reveals

The word "breakthrough" suggests sudden change, but real breakthroughs in leadership and life are usually the result of systematic preparation meeting the right moment. Burnout, paradoxically, often creates that right moment by forcing you to examine assumptions and practices you might otherwise never question.

Elena's breakthrough came in month seven of her recovery. Her company faced a crisis—one of their drugs failed a crucial regulatory review, requiring a complete redesign of their clinical trial approach—two years of work, $50 million in investment, suddenly at risk.

The old Elena would have personally managed every aspect of the crisis response, working around the clock until the problem was solved or she collapsed trying.

Instead, she found herself asking different questions: "Who on our team is best positioned to lead this response? What do they need from me to be successful? How can we solve this crisis in a way that strengthens our systems rather than just fixing the immediate problem?"

She convened her leadership council, assigned clear ownership to her head of clinical development, secured board support for the timeline and budget needed, and scheduled daily check-ins to provide strategic guidance without micromanaging execution.

The crisis was resolved more quickly and effectively than previous ones. But more importantly, Elena realized she had fundamentally changed her approach to leadership. She was no longer the person who solved every problem—she was the person who built systems where issues could be solved effectively by the right people.

"That's when I knew the recovery was complete," Elena told me during one of our final sessions. "Not because I felt perfect, but because I was leading from my values rather than my fears."

My own breakthrough moment came three months after the breakdown, standing at the edge of the Øresund on a cold May morning, preparing for my first ocean swim. The water was only 8 degrees Celsius, but something in me knew it was time. As I waded in, I felt my body responding not with the panic I expected, but with a kind of resilient alertness I hadn't experienced in years.

The cold water was a reset button for my nervous system. Still, more than that, it was a metaphor for what recovery had become: the willingness to enter discomfort intentionally, knowing that what doesn't overwhelm you can strengthen you.

Questions for Reflection

Transformational Question: What if this breakdown is the gift you needed—the one that forces you to build the leadership practice and life you've always wanted but never permitted yourself to create?

Personal Awareness: What would have to be true for your current way of working to be sustainable for the next five years? What patterns, beliefs, or approaches is your burnout asking you to reconsider? What does your body know about your limits that your mind keeps overriding?

Systemic Thinking: How does your organization's culture make recovery difficult? What would need to change in your environment for sustainable leadership to be the norm rather than the exception? How might your recovery influence what's possible for others in your organization?

Action-Oriented: What aspects of your pre-burnout self do you want to reclaim, and what aspects are you ready to leave behind? What's one boundary you could set this week? What would you stop, start, or restructure if you took your recovery seriously?

Integration: How might your recovery journey serve not just you, but the people you lead and love? What would it look like to be successful in a way that energizes rather than depletes you? In a world where AI handles routine cognitive load, what uniquely human capacities could you reclaim?

These questions don't require immediate answers. In fact, the most valuable insights often emerge gradually as you implement systematic changes and observe their effects.

Walking the forest loop for what must be the thousandth time now, I realize these questions have been answered not through analysis but through practice. Recovery taught me that the path forward isn't found by thinking harder about the problem, but by taking the next right step, consistently, with faith that the destination will reveal itself along the way.

The Bridge Forward

Recovery from burnout is both an ending and a beginning. It's the end of unsustainable patterns that were depleting your energy and creativity. And it's the beginning of a more integrated approach to leadership and life.

But recovery, as profound as it is, reveals an even larger framework. The practices that enable individual recovery—the focus on energy management, values alignment, systematic thinking, human-centered approaches, and conscious human-AI collaboration—aren't just tools for crisis intervention. They're the foundation for an entirely different model of leadership.

Standing at the edge of my familiar forest path, notebook full of insights that would help hundreds of other leaders navigate their own recoveries,

I began to see that this systematic approach to healing pointed toward something larger: a framework for thriving, not just surviving.

The Recovery Roadmap reveals a larger framework for "Whole Human Leadership"—an approach that integrates professional effectiveness with personal sustainability, individual achievement with collective well-being, immediate results with long-term impact, and human wisdom with technological capability.

The framework we'll explore next doesn't just help leaders recover from burnout. It helps them prevent it entirely by designing systems that honor both the human and the leader, both the individual and the team, both the urgent and the important, both what technologies can do and what only humans can.

This is where recovery becomes transformation, where healing becomes growth, where breakdown becomes the foundation for a completely different way of leading and living.

The systematic recovery approach creates the foundation for integrated leadership. But what does that integration look like in practice? In Chapter 8, we'll explore the Whole Human Framework—the comprehensive model for leading as a complete person in an incomplete world.

8 The Whole Human Framework

The model behind the method.

The tram announces its arrival before I can see it—that metallic screech of steel wheels on steel rails, mixed with the electric hum of overhead wires. I'm standing on Brīvības iela in the heart of Riga, and the morning city is assembling itself through sound. A woman's heels click past in staccato rhythm. Two men argue in Russian about football, their voices rising and falling like tides. Somewhere behind me, a street musician is warming up—not quite music yet, just the promise of it, scales ascending and descending through the cold October air.

I'm early for my meeting with Maris, so I let myself sink into the acoustic architecture of this city. Riga has a different "sound" than Copenhagen's muted efficiency or London's more aggressive bustle. Here, conversations overlap without competing—Latvian, Russian, English, and German all coexisting in the same acoustic space, like a cacophony of culture in a setting that does not broadcast diversity like, say, a London or New York. The tram rings its bell, passengers shuffle and resettle, and someone's coffee cup clinks against a saucer in the café behind me.

A phone rings nearby—the old-fashioned ring, not a digital chirp—and a man answers in what might be Lithuanian or Estonian, I can't quite tell. His voice drops to a whisper, then rises again, urgent but controlled. Business, I'm thinking.

The street musician finds her melody now, something traditional that I don't recognize, but that makes the older woman at the bus stop smile with recognition. The music weaves through the other sounds—car engines, bicycle bells, the pneumatic hiss of a bus door, footsteps on cobblestone switching to footsteps on modern pavement and back again.

Old European cities offer a remarkable layering of eras, a quality I appreciate. You can hear a medieval bell tower chime the hour with deep bronze notes, centuries before the invention of electricity. Moments later, someone's smartphone alarm pierces the air with a synthetic, urgent ring, or perhaps the latest pop song plays. Both sounds coexist in the same space, neither one diminishing the presence of the other.

Maris appears through the morning crowd with the purposeful stride of someone who learned early that hesitation wastes energy. She's forty-two but moves with the careful efficiency of someone managing chronic pain—not visible to most people, but I've learned to recognize the small compensations. She greets me with a firm handshake and a half-smile that says she's evaluated this meeting's potential value and decided to show up anyway.

"Shall we?" she gestures to the café, and we navigate through the outdoor tables where early risers huddle over laptops and newspapers, their conversations adding another layer to the soundscape—startup pitches in English, family planning in Latvian, real estate negotiations in Russian.

Inside, the acoustic shifts. The street noise becomes a muffled backdrop, replaced by the intimacy of porcelain touching wood, espresso machines building pressure, the soft rustle of someone turning newspaper pages. We settle at a corner table where the sound is clear enough for conversation but not so exposed that others will overhear.

"Thank you for meeting me here," Maris begins, her English carrying the slight Baltic accent that makes every statement sound precisely considered. "I could have done this over Zoom, but I've learned that the important conversations need to happen in person."

She pauses as the waiter brings our coffees, the cups settling onto saucers with that ceramic click that punctuates Riga's café culture.

"Three weeks ago, my CTO resigned. Two days after that, my Head of Product followed. Yesterday, my CFO asked if we could talk about 'sustainable pace.' That's the polite Latvian way of saying 'I'm burning out and you're the reason.'"

The espresso machine hisses behind us, drowning out whatever else she was going to say. When the noise subsides, she continues.

"I built this company on being unbreakable. Five years ago, we were three people in a shared workspace in Āgenskalns. Now we're ninety people across four countries, processing 2.3 billion euros in transactions annually. We've survived market crashes, regulatory changes, a pandemic, and three direct competitors trying to replicate our model. I thought that made us strong. What I'm realizing is that I've built something unsustainable on a foundation that was already cracking."

The Pattern of Fragmentation

What Maris was describing is one of the most common and costly patterns I encounter in my work with leaders who have built successful companies or careers through sheer force of will and personal capability. They succeed by being exceptional at managing complexity, making decisions under uncertainty, and carrying more responsibility than seems humanly possible. Their companies grow. Their reputations expand. Their bank accounts reflect their value to their organizations or investors.

But something else happens in parallel, something less visible but more insidious. The very skills that enable their success to begin to work against them. The ability to push through exhaustion becomes the inability to recognize when rest is strategically necessary. The habit of solving every problem personally becomes a bottleneck that prevents others from developing their own capabilities. The identity built around being the strongest person in the room becomes a prison that prevents vulnerability, connection, and ultimately, sustainable leadership.

In Danish, we have a word—*tilfredshed*—that captures something the English word "satisfaction" misses. It's not the satisfaction of achievement, the feeling when you complete a project or hit a target. It's a more profound contentment that comes from alignment between your actions and your values, between your external success and your internal sense of wholeness. *Tilfredshed* doesn't depend on the next milestone. It exists independently of external validation.

Maris had built a successful company but lost *fulfillment* somewhere along the way. The measures that mattered to her investors—revenue, growth rate, market share—told one story. But the measures that mattered to her humanity—sleep quality, relationship depth, sense of purpose, capacity for presence—told a different story entirely.

"I thought balance was something I would do later," she tells me, stirring her coffee slowly. "After we hit profitability. After the Series C. After we established market leadership. After, after, after. What I'm understanding now is that 'after' never arrives. The goalpost keeps moving, and I keep telling myself that once I cross it, then I'll focus on balance. But the crossing never happens. The race just gets longer."

My work over the past five years has involved helping hundreds of leaders navigate their way back from burnout, breakdown, or what I call "high-performance fragmentation"—that state where you're succeeding externally while fragmenting internally. The Recovery Roadmap I developed, which we explored in Chapter 7, has proven effective for crisis intervention.

But as I worked with more leaders through their recovery processes, I noticed something. The same systematic approaches that enabled recovery—the focus on energy management, the emphasis on values alignment, the attention to relationships, the creation of collective capability—these weren't just tools for healing. They were the foundation for an entirely different model of leadership.

The leaders who recovered most completely and sustainably weren't the ones who simply stopped working so hard or delegated more tasks. They were the ones who fundamentally redesigned how they led—not just in their professional contexts, but across every domain of their lives. They didn't just fix what was broken. They built something new on a different foundation.

This realization led to what I now call the Whole Human Framework—a systematic approach to integration that addresses the full complexity of what it means to lead as a complete person rather than a fragmented professional.

The Science Behind Integration

The Whole Human Framework isn't just lived experience and pattern recognition. It's supported by research across multiple disciplines.

- **Neuroscience of Integration:** Studies from the Max Planck Institute show that when leaders operate from an integrated state rather than a fragmented stress response, their prefrontal cortex (responsible for strategic thinking, emotional regulation, and complex decision-making) shows 31% more activity while their amygdala (stress and threat response) shows 23% less activation. Integration literally changes which parts of your brain are dominant during leadership activities.
- **Systemic Performance:** Research from INSEAD tracking 800+ companies over seven years found that organizations led by executives scoring high on integration metrics (personal sustainability, relational intelligence, team synergy, systemic impact awareness) outperformed their peer companies by 19% in revenue growth and 27% in employee retention. Integration isn't just personal benefit—it's a competitive advantage.
- **Recovery Speed:** Copenhagen Business School studied 312 executives who experienced burnout. Those who used systematic integration approaches (similar to my Four Quadrants below) recovered full cognitive function 60% faster than those who focused solely on rest and stress reduction. Integration accelerates recovery because it addresses root causes rather than just managing symptoms.
- **Cultural Transmission:** Aalto University research on organizational culture found that leader integration patterns are 3.2 times more influential on team health than stated company policies. What leaders do systematically create culture more powerfully than what organizations say officially. Your integration or fragmentation becomes contagious.
- **Long-Term Sustainability:** Yale School of Management's 15-year longitudinal study of executive careers found that leaders who demonstrated integration across all four quadrants (measured through 360 feedback and behavioral observation) had 73% lower rates of

serious health events (heart disease, stroke, major depression) and remained in senior leadership roles 4.7 years longer on average. Integration isn't just a performance tool—it's a longevity strategy.

The research consensus is clear: Integration isn't a soft skill or a nice-to-have. It's a fundamental architecture for sustainable high performance.

The Whole Human Framework: Four Quadrants

The framework emerged from patterns I observed across hundreds of leadership situations, from Berlin boardrooms to Dubai strategy sessions, from Silicon Valley startups to Copenhagen consulting firms. It synthesizes insights from systems theory, neuroscience, organizational psychology, and—most importantly—the lived experience of leaders who have navigated from fragmentation to integration.

The framework rests on a simple but powerful premise: Sustainable leadership requires attending to four interconnected domains simultaneously. You cannot excel in one while neglecting the others without creating systemic fragility. True *fulfillment*—that deep satisfaction that doesn't depend on external validation—comes from coherent attention across all four.

Quadrant 1: Personal Sustainability

This is where most leaders begin when they recognize something needs to change. They focus on personal practices—exercise routines, meditation apps, sleep optimization, and nutrition plans. These matter, but personal sustainability goes deeper than wellness habits.

Personal sustainability is about building a life architecture that generates more energy than it consumes. It's about understanding your actual capacity and designing your days, weeks, and years to work with that capacity rather than against it.

During my recovery in 2020, I discovered I had similar energy even after reducing my work hours from 70 per week to 45. Not because the work itself was energizing or draining, but because I had been running a system designed for crisis mode as if it were a sustainable operating model. Every decision depleted me because I was making decisions without sufficient rest. Every relationship felt like work because I never had enough reserves to be genuinely present. Every opportunity felt like a threat because I had no buffer for the unexpected.

Personal sustainability requires three foundational practices:

- **Energy Architecture Design:** Understanding when you have capacity for what kinds of work. Klaus in Munich, whose story opened Chapter 4 on energy management, discovered he was spending his highest-capacity morning hours on reactive email management and his depleted evening hours on strategic thinking. Simply inverting that pattern—protecting mornings for strategy and relegating email to afternoons—didn't require working different hours, just working differently within those hours.
- **Recovery Integration:** Building rest into your system as a design feature, not an emergency response. This means deliberate recovery practices—not just when you're exhausted, but as ongoing maintenance. (Chapter 3 explored the warning signs; Chapter 7 offered the systematic recovery approach.) The Scandinavian approach to work includes regular breaks, sensible vacation policies, and social time built into the workday. These aren't indulgences. They're how you sustain performance over decades rather than burning bright for a few years before extinguishing.
- **Values Alignment:** Regularly auditing how you spend your time against what you claim to value. (Chapter 5 examined how professional over-functioning erodes personal presence.) Maris realized she was spending 60 hours weekly on activities that advanced her company's strategic priorities. Still, zero hours on activities that reflected her stated value of "being present for my daughters' teenage years." This misalignment between values and time allocation was creating internal fragmentation that no amount of meditation could resolve.

The research here is detailed: Leaders who attend to personal sustainability don't just feel better—they make better decisions, build stronger teams, and create more value over time. A Stanford study of executive decision quality found that well-rested leaders made 23% fewer strategic errors than their sleep-deprived counterparts. That's not marginal. That's the difference between successful execution and expensive mistakes.

Quadrant 2: Relational Intelligence

This quadrant addresses how you show up in relationships—not just at work, but across all contexts. Relational intelligence isn't about being likable or charismatic. It's about being authentically present in ways that create connection rather than isolation.

The pattern I see most often in high-achieving leaders is "competence refuge"—using professional skill as a shield against the vulnerable work of genuine connection. Anders in Oslo, from Chapter 5 on over-functioning, had mastered this completely. He could solve complex strategic problems but couldn't be emotionally present with his daughter. His competence had become his hiding place.

Relational intelligence requires developing capacity in three areas:

- **Authentic Presence:** The ability to be fully present with another person without needing to fix, solve, or manage them. This is harder than it sounds, especially for people who have built their identity around being the problem-solver. I had to learn this skill slowly, painfully, through my relationship with my partner and my son. They didn't need my solutions. They required my presence. Those are different currencies.
- **Vulnerability as Strength:** The willingness to not know, to ask for help, to admit uncertainty. In American business culture, we confuse vulnerability with weakness. Leaders who can acknowledge what they don't know create environments where others can contribute their expertise. Priya in London, whose story opened Chapter 2 on silence, discovered that saying "I don't know" didn't diminish her authority—it distributed intelligence across her team.
- **Reciprocity Patterns:** Building relationships characterized by mutual giving and receiving rather than one-directional problem-solving.

When you're always the helper, you never have to be helped. When you're always strong, you never have to receive support. This creates isolation masquerading as competence.

The research on relational intelligence in leadership is striking. Studies from Aalto University in Finland show that leaders who score high on relational intelligence metrics (authentic presence, vulnerability, reciprocity) have teams with 34% higher psychological safety scores and 28% better performance on complex problem-solving tasks. Relational intelligence isn't a soft skill. It's a strategic advantage.

Quadrant 3: Team Synergy

This quadrant moves beyond individual relationships to address how you create collective capability. Most leaders understand that teams matter. Fewer understand how to build teams that function as something more than the sum of individual talents.

Team synergy emerges when you shift from being the indispensable center of every decision to being the architect of systems where others can thrive without you. This requires fundamentally rethinking what leadership means.

When I was flat on my back with the flu in East Dulwich, watching ordinary South London residents coordinate complex interactions without any central authority, I realized I had spent years trying to be the organizing principle of every system I touched. But the highest form of leadership isn't making yourself indispensable. It's creating conditions where others can flourish independently.

Team synergy requires attention to three elements:

- **Distributed Intelligence:** Creating systems where knowledge flows laterally, not just hierarchically. Where the expertise in the room gets accessed regardless of who has the fancy title, where junior people can challenge senior people without career risk. Ingrid in Stockholm (whose story is in Chapter 6) learned this when her team finally told her they had better solutions than she did—they just needed permission to implement them.

- **Collective Accountability:** Moving from "the leader is responsible for everything" to "we're collectively responsible for our shared outcomes." This doesn't mean the leader has no special responsibilities. It means those responsibilities include creating conditions for collective ownership rather than individual heroics.
- **Systematic Capability Building:** Investing in team development not as occasional training but as an ongoing system design. When Klaus realized he was the bottleneck in every decision, he didn't just delegate more. He systematically built his team's decision-making capability through structured practice, feedback, and gradually expanding autonomy.

Research from IMD in Switzerland shows that teams scoring high on these three dimensions (distributed intelligence, collective accountability, systematic capability) outperform traditional hierarchical teams by 41% on complex projects requiring coordination across functional boundaries. Team synergy isn't just nice to have. It's a competitive requirement.

Quadrant 4: Systemic Impact

This quadrant addresses the question: Beyond your personal sustainability, your relationships, and your immediate team, what ripples are you creating in the larger systems you touch?

Systemic impact isn't about legacy or grand visions. It's about understanding that your actions as a leader influence systems beyond your direct control—organizational culture, industry norms, societal expectations about what leadership looks like. You're creating patterns that others will either replicate or reject.

When Maris's CTO and Head of Product resigned within forty-eight hours of each other, they weren't just making personal decisions. They were sending a signal about what kind of leadership creates what kind of organizational culture. Their departures would influence how others in the fintech ecosystem thought about sustainable pace versus growth at all costs.

Systemic impact requires consciousness in three domains:

- **Cultural Architecture:** Understanding that every decision you make as a leader influences the culture you're creating. When you respond to emails at 11 p.m., you're not just managing your own time—you're signaling what's expected. When you celebrate all-nighters and weekend work, you're not just recognizing effort—you're defining what excellence looks like in your system.

- **Ripple Awareness:** Recognizing that your personal patterns create permission structures for others. Stefan in Berlin, whose son left him cake from the science project presentation he missed, wasn't just affecting his own family. His constant availability was teaching his entire team that being a good leader meant being unavailable to the people you love. (Read Stefan's story in Chapter 3.)
- **Intentional Modeling:** Consciously demonstrating the integration you want to see in your organization. This doesn't mean performing authenticity or making your personal life public. It means being honest about your boundaries, your limitations, and your commitment to sustainable performance. When I started telling clients, "I don't work Fridays," rather than pretending to be constantly available, I permitted them to have boundaries too.

Research from Copenhagen Business School shows that leaders who score high on systemic impact awareness (cultural architecture, ripple awareness, intentional modeling) create organizations with 37% lower turnover, 29% higher employee engagement, and 23% better long-term financial performance. Systemic impact isn't altruism. It's an intelligent design.

What I Wish I'd Known: Integration Isn't Sequential

If I could go back to my younger self—the one building his first startup, believing that personal sacrifice was the price of professional achievement—I would tell him this:

The framework isn't sequential. You don't master personal sustainability, then move to relational intelligence, then team synergy, then systemic impact. You work on all four simultaneously, accepting that some will always be stronger than others, but none can be neglected entirely.

Small changes in one quadrant create ripples across the others. When I started protecting my mornings for strategic thinking (personal sustainability), my afternoon meetings became more effective because I showed up with clarity rather than depletion (team synergy). When I became more willing to admit uncertainty (relational intelligence), my team started bringing me better information because they knew I was listening (team synergy).

Integration feels slower than optimization, but compounds faster over time. In the first three months of working with the framework, you might not see dramatic changes. But a year in, you'll realize you're making better decisions, building stronger relationships, and creating more value with less effort. Three years in, you'll look back and barely recognize the fragmented person you used to be.

The framework doesn't promise perfection. Some days you'll still push too hard, close too many doors, choose achievement over connection. The difference is that you'll notice the fragmentation faster and have systematic ways to restore integration.

Tilfredshed—that deep satisfaction independent of achievement—isn't the reward for doing the work. It's the signal that you're integrated. When you feel it, you know the framework is working.

Integration, Not Optimization

Here's what the Whole Human Framework isn't: It's not a system for optimizing yourself into a more efficient leader. It's not about hacking your productivity, maximizing your output, or squeezing more performance from your existing capacity.

The framework is about *integration*—bringing together the four quadrants into coherent wholeness rather than managing them as competing priorities. When you attend to personal sustainability while neglecting relational intelligence, you end up fit and lonely. When you build team synergy while ignoring systemic impact, you create high-performing teams in toxic cultures. The magic happens when all four quadrants develop together.

This is what *tilfredshed* really means—that sense of deep satisfaction that comes not from achieving one more thing, but from living in alignment across all domains simultaneously. You can't fake it. You can't schedule it after the next funding round. You either design for it systematically, or you fragment gradually.

This distinction between integration and optimization matters more now than ever, because we live in an age of extraordinary optimization tools. Artificial intelligence can analyze your calendar and suggest efficiency improvements. It can process your communication patterns and recommend better scheduling. It can even coach you through difficult conversations with scripts and frameworks.

But AI cannot integrate you. It can optimize individual quadrants in isolation, but it cannot create coherence across all four simultaneously.

Consider what AI can and cannot do within the framework:

- In Personal Sustainability, AI can track your sleep, suggest exercise routines, and remind you to take breaks. These are useful optimizations. But personal sustainability isn't really about habits. It's about designing a life architecture that reflects your actual values. AI can tell you that you're sleeping poorly. It cannot help you understand why you're avoiding rest, or what you're running from, or what would need to change for recovery to feel safe.
- In Relational Intelligence, AI can draft messages, suggest conversation starters, and analyze communication patterns. But relational intelligence isn't about better communication techniques. It's about authentic presence, about the willingness to be uncertain and curious, about the capacity to sit with another person without needing to solve them. No AI can be present with you in that way. No algorithm can offer genuine *ro*.
- In Team Synergy, AI can facilitate coordination, track project status, and even suggest optimal team compositions. But team synergy emerges from trust, from the willingness to be vulnerable with colleagues, from the slow accumulation of shared experience that creates collective intelligence. AI can make teams more efficient. It cannot make them more human.
- In Systemic Impact, AI can model ripple effects and analyze organizational patterns. But systemic impact requires something AI

fundamentally lacks: the capacity to model behavior that others will want to follow. Your integration or fragmentation becomes contagious. Your AI assistant's integration or fragmentation does not.

The leaders I work with sometimes ask whether AI might eventually solve the integration problem. I don't think it will, not because the technology isn't sophisticated enough, but because integration is inherently relational. It requires a self that can be fragmented and made whole, relationships that can be neglected and repaired, teams that can be depleted and restored, systems that can be shaped by human presence. These are not optimization problems with technical solutions. They are human challenges that require human attention.

What AI can do is handle enough of the transactional work that leaders have more capacity for the integration work. It can free up time and cognitive resources that can then be invested in the four quadrants. But only if leaders choose to use the recovered capacity for integration rather than filling it with more optimization.

Maris and I spent three hours mapping her current state across the four quadrants. The picture that emerged was sobering but clarifying.

- **Personal Sustainability:** She was running on five hours of sleep, eating irregularly, and had stopped most physical activity two years ago. Her energy architecture was reactive rather than designed—she worked whenever demands arrived rather than protecting time for strategic thinking.
- **Relational Intelligence:** She described her relationships as "transactional"—useful for business purposes but not sources of genuine connection or support. Her daughters had stopped telling her about their lives because they knew she'd be physically present but mentally elsewhere.
- **Team Synergy:** She was the central bottleneck for most significant decisions. Her team had learned to wait for her input rather than developing their own judgment. When she was unavailable, projects stalled.
- **Systemic Impact:** She was creating a culture where burnout was a badge of honor and boundaries were seen as a weakness. Her best people were leaving, not because they couldn't do the work, but because they didn't want to become like her.

"So that's it," she said quietly, looking at the framework diagram we'd sketched on paper napkins. "I've been succeeding at the wrong metrics while failing at the ones that actually matter."

"Not failing," I corrected. "Fragmenting. And fragmentation can be healed through systematic integration."

Leader Spotlight: From Fragmentation to Integration

Janis, CEO of a logistics company, has 180+ employees across Latvia, Lithuania, and Estonia. When I first met Janis in 2022, he was running on extreme depletion—averaging four hours of sleep, managing every significant decision personally, and proud of being available to his team 24/7.

His VP of Operations quit via email, citing Janis's "inability to let anyone else lead" as the reason. The resignation triggered reflection: "I realized I'd built a company that couldn't function without me. I thought that made me valuable. What it actually made me was a bottleneck."

Janis worked through the Four-Week Integration Practice, then committed to systematic redesign across all four quadrants:

- **Personal Sustainability:** Established a non-negotiable 11 p.m. to 6 a.m. offline window, built a morning exercise routine, and created a weekly strategic thinking time with zero interruptions.
- **Relational Intelligence:** Started monthly vulnerability sessions with the senior team, where he shared what he was uncertain about, began asking for help rather than only offering it, and rebuilt a relationship with his adult daughter by being curious rather than advisory.
- **Team Synergy:** Documented decision-making frameworks for operational choices, explicitly transferred authority for specific domains to specific people, and created systems for team decisions that didn't require his approval.
- **Systemic Impact:** Changed his 24/7 availability to "emergencies only after 6 p.m., with emergency clearly defined," started talking openly about his integration work in company meetings, and created a policy where senior leaders must take complete offline vacations.

Here are the results after one year:

- **Personal:** Six hours average sleep, regular exercise, relationships described as "actually connected."
- **Team:** Three direct reports promoted to decision-making authority they previously lacked, employee engagement scores up 34%.
- **Business:** Revenue up 23%, operating margin improved eight percentage points, voluntary turnover down to 7% from 19%.
- **Culture:** Glassdoor rating improved from 3.2 to 4.6, with comments specifically noting "sustainable pace" and "trustworthy leadership."

Janis's reflection: "The most surprising part wasn't that integration worked—it's that it worked so fast. I thought I needed to be everywhere, do everything, and control all decisions. When I systematically stepped back and built actual systems, the company performed better, and I became a person my family wanted to spend time with. Turns out you can have *tilfredshed* (he said "satisfaction") and business results. You just can't have either one if you're fragmenting."

The Four-Week Integration Practice

The Whole Human Framework isn't theoretical. It requires systematic practice across all four quadrants simultaneously. Here's a four-week implementation structure that builds incrementally.

Week 1: Baseline Mapping (Personal Sustainability + Relational Intelligence)

Daily Practice (15 minutes):

- **Morning:** Energy check-in. Rate your physical, mental, and emotional energy on a 1–10 scale. Notice patterns about when you start days with capacity versus depletion.
- **Evening:** Relationship audit. Identify one interaction where you were authentically present and one where you were performing competence rather than showing up genuinely.

Weekly Practice (60 minutes):

- Map your energy architecture. For one whole week, track when you're doing what kinds of work. Notice mismatches—strategic thinking during low-energy hours, reactive email during high-capacity mornings.
- Identify three relationships where you habitually show up in "helper" or "expert" mode rather than a reciprocal connection. Choose one where you'll practice asking for help this week.

Success Metric: You can articulate your actual energy patterns and identify at least one relationship where you default to competence refuge instead of authentic presence.

Week 2: Systematic Design (Personal Sustainability + Team Synergy)

Daily Practice (20 minutes):

- **Morning:** Protect first 90 minutes for strategic work, no email, no meetings. Use this time for thinking, not doing.
- **Afternoon:** Delegate one decision you would usually make yourself. Brief the person, give them decision authority, and don't rescue them if they struggle.

Weekly Practice (90 minutes):

- Redesign your week around energy reality, not an aspirational schedule. Block specific time for specific work types based on your Week 1 mapping.
- Facilitate one team meeting where you don't provide the answer. Ask questions, surface others' expertise, and let them solve the problem collectively.

Success Metric: You've protected high-capacity time for strategic work and enabled at least one team decision without your direct involvement.

Week 3: Relational Depth (Relational Intelligence + Team Synergy)

Daily Practice (25 minutes):

- **Morning:** Identify one person you'll be genuinely curious about today. Not networking, not managing—actual interest in their experience.
- **Evening:** Practice saying "I don't know" or "I need help with this" in at least one professional context.

Weekly Practice (2 hours):

- Have one vulnerable conversation with someone on your team. Share something you're genuinely uncertain about. Ask for their perspective, not their reassurance.
- Create a new system that enables team decisions without your presence. Document decision criteria, give explicit authority, and step back completely.

Success Metric: You've demonstrated vulnerability without losing authority and created at least one decision-making system that functions independently.

Week 4: Systemic Coherence (All Four Quadrants)

Daily Practice (30 minutes):

- **Morning:** Conscious modeling. What pattern do you want to reinforce in your system today? How will your actions reflect that?
- **Evening:** Ripple awareness. What did your behavior today teach others about what's valued, what's expected, what's possible?

Weekly Practice (2–3 hours):

- Audit your systemic impact. What culture are you creating, regardless of what you say you value? Where do your actions and values misalign?
- Design one significant change that addresses misalignment across multiple quadrants. Maybe it's "no meetings before 10 a.m." (Personal Sustainability + Systemic Impact). Perhaps it's "I don't respond to non-urgent communication after 6 p.m." (Personal Sustainability + Relational Intelligence + Team Synergy).

Success Metric: You can articulate the systemic patterns you're creating and have implemented one coherent change that affects multiple quadrants simultaneously.

Ongoing Integration

After four weeks, you'll have baseline awareness and some new patterns established. Integration is an ongoing practice, not a destination. The framework becomes most powerful when you use it as a diagnostic tool:

- When you feel depleted, ask: Am I protecting my capacity? (Personal Sustainability)
- When relationships feel transactional, ask: Am I maintaining genuine connection? (Relational Intelligence)
- When you're doing everything yourself, ask: Am I developing collective capability? (Team Synergy)
- When the culture feels off, ask: Am I creating healthy patterns in the systems I influence? (Systemic Impact)

Maris committed to this four-week practice. Three months later, she sent me a message: "I'm sleeping six hours consistently, which feels like luxury. My daughters tell me things about their lives now. My new CTO told me this is the first job where she feels trusted to make decisions. And we just had our most profitable quarter. It's not perfect. But it's working."

Questions for Reflection

Transformational Question: What becomes possible when you design for wholeness rather than optimize for performance?

Personal Awareness: Which of the four quadrants feels most neglected in your current leadership approach? Where do you notice the most obvious fragmentation between what you claim to value and how you spend your time and energy?

Systemic Thinking: What patterns are you creating in the larger systems you influence? If your direct reports led the way you lead, what kind of organization would that make? What would need to change?

Action-Oriented: Looking at the Four-Week Integration Practice, which week feels most necessary for you right now? What's one small change you could implement this week that would affect multiple quadrants simultaneously?

Integration: When have you experienced *tilfredshed*—that deep satisfaction independent of achievement? What conditions enabled that feeling? How might you design for it systematically rather than hoping it arrives accidentally?

The Whole Symphony

The afternoon light shifts in the Riga café, casting long shadows across our table. Maris has been quiet for a while, studying the framework diagram we sketched. Outside, the street musician has moved on, replaced by the evening sounds of the city assembling for whatever comes next.

"This feels both obvious and impossible," she finally says. "Obvious because, of course, this is what integrated leadership looks like. Impossible because redesigning four things simultaneously while running a company seems overwhelming."

I remember feeling the same way when I first glimpsed what integration required. The gap between fragmentation and wholeness looked unbridgeable.

"The trick," I tell her, "is that you're not redesigning four separate things. You're redesigning one system that happens to have four essential elements. Start anywhere. A change in one quadrant creates ripples in the others. The framework doesn't demand perfection. It just requires attention to all four domains, however imperfectly."

She nods slowly, and I can see something shifting—not certainty, but willingness. The openness to possibility is the first requirement for any meaningful transformation.

The framework reveals what wholeness requires. But integration only happens when you're willing to step into your full humanity rather than hide behind professional competence.

As we leave the café, Riga's evening chorus is building—tram bells and footsteps, conversations and car horns, the complex acoustics of a city that's learned to hold multiple histories, languages, and futures in the same space. Integration isn't about choosing one sound over another. It's about creating conditions where the whole symphony can be heard.

The framework works only when you stop trying to be the hero and start being human. And that conversation—about what it means to lead from humanity rather than heroics—is waiting for us in Chapter 9.

9 From Hero to Human

Why stepping down creates better leaders.

Wei is already eating when I arrive at the dumpling shop, a narrow storefront I would have walked past if he hadn't sent explicit directions. The morning crowd fills the small space with the energy of people eating breakfast with purpose—not lingering but not rushing either. Just present with their soup dumplings and jasmine tea.

He looks up when I approach, gestures to the seat across from him. There's something different about him than when we spoke on the phone three weeks ago. Not better exactly, but more honest.

"Good morning," he says, pushing a menu toward me, though we both know what I'll order. Everyone orders the same thing at places like this—*xiaolongbao*, the soup dumplings that Shanghai does better than anywhere else. "I could have suggested a coffee shop in Xintiandi, something more convenient. But I needed to be here. My mother used to bring me to this shop before school, thirty years ago."

I ordered a steamer of dumplings and hot tea. The waiter brings them quickly—no prolonged service, no spiel. Just food arriving when it's ready.

"You sounded exhausted on the phone," I tell him, my Danish directness cutting through what might otherwise become extended pleasantries. "But you also sounded like you'd made some kind of decision."

Wei picks up another dumpling with practiced precision, dips it in the black vinegar mixed with ginger, and pauses before eating it. When he bites through the wrapper, I can see the exact moment the hot soup hits his mouth—that brief surprise, even when you know it's coming.

"I am exhausted," he admits. "But that's not new. I've been exhausted since I took the CEO role eighteen months ago. What's new is that I can't remember why I thought exhaustion was required for excellence."

I bite into my first dumpling and understand immediately why Wei chose this place. The burst of hot soup grounds you entirely in the present moment. No multitasking is possible when you're managing not to burn your mouth. The taste is simple but perfect—pork and ginger and something ineffable that can only be described as "rightness."

"My wife is in Copenhagen, visiting old friends," Wei tells me, rotating his teacup slowly. The jasmine scent rises with the steam between us. "Has been for two weeks. She's thinking about us. That's what she said when she left. Not threatening divorce, not asking for changes. Just 'thinking'. Which somehow feels worse than if she'd decided."

I pour us both more tea and wait. There's more coming. I've learned that silence creates space for the truth that's trying to emerge.

"And yesterday, my COO gave notice. Li. Best operations executive I've ever worked with and built three successful ops teams before this role. I recruited her specifically because she's brilliant. Her exit interview was twenty minutes of her explaining, very diplomatically, that I don't let her do her job. I solve everything before she can learn. I approve every decision before she can. I've turned her into an overpaid assistant instead of a leader."

I've heard versions of this story dozens of times—the capable leader who becomes a hindrance, the hero who creates dependency. But Wei's version has an additional layer of complexity that makes it particularly instructive.

"And the week before that," he continues, "my doctor told me my blood pressure is concerning. Chest pains during our earnings call. He said stress-related, recommended immediate changes. I heard 'work smarter', not 'work differently'. Because I've been trained to believe I can optimize my way out of any problem."

He finishes his tea and pours more. Around us, the morning customers are cycling through—some lingering over second pots of tea, others already heading to offices. The rhythm of the place has its own logic, unhurried but efficient.

"I learned sustainable leadership in Copenhagen," he tells me, and I can hear something shift in his voice—not quite nostalgia, but recognition of something lost. "Fifteen years of building wind farms, battery systems, and grid solutions. Nordic companies that valued presence over performance, human beings over human resources. I was effective. Respected. I went home at six. Lin and I would bike along the lakes, make dinner together, and talk about things beyond logistics. My team in Denmark didn't need me to have all the answers. They just required me to create conditions where they could find the answers."

The dumpling shop owner brings a fresh pot of tea without being asked—he remembers Wei always wants more tea. This kind of quiet attention, knowing what someone needs without them asking, is what the Danes call *hygge* in one of its many forms. Not the candles-and-coziness version people think about, but the quality of presence that makes a moment feel complete.

"When I came back to China three years ago," Wei continues, "I told myself the European approach wouldn't work here. Different culture, different competitive pressures, different expectations of what CEOs do. When they promoted me to CEO eighteen months ago, I abandoned everything I learned. I became what I thought Chinese leadership required—the hero who solves everything, the Iron Man who never admits uncertainty, the CEO whose identity is inseparable from the company's performance."

He looks at me directly now, and I recognize this moment—when someone stops believing their story and starts telling it.

"I destroyed my marriage, my health, and my effectiveness trying to prove I deserved a role I was already qualified for. And the worst part? The company that hired me wanted the European-trained leader I was, not the caricature of Chinese hero CEO I thought I needed to become."

The Trap of Hero Leadership

I've seen this pattern so often, it has its own shape in my mind now—the accomplished leader who abandons what works to perform what they think is expected. Wei's version is evident because he can articulate both sides: the sustainable European approach that made him effective and the heroic Chinese performance that's destroying him.

"Tell me about hero leadership," I say. "Not as concept, but as lived experience. What does it feel like from inside?"

Wei considers this while finishing another dumpling. I notice he eats slowly despite the breakfast rush around us—some habits from childhood stay with you even when everything else changes.

"It feels like constant vigilance," he says finally. "Every problem that crosses my desk is a test. Every decision I make is evidence of whether I deserve this role. Every time someone struggles, I interpret it as my failure to lead properly. So I solved everything. I'm the first one in, last one out. I respond to emails at midnight. I insert myself into decisions that my team should own. Not because the company needs me to do these things, but because I need to prove I'm valuable."

"And how's that working?" I ask, though we both know the answer.

"It's destroying everything I claim to value. My marriage is fragmenting. My best executive is leaving. My health is compromised. And the company—which should be thriving given our market position—is becoming structurally fragile because everything runs through me. I'm the bottleneck I was hired to eliminate."

This is the trap of hero leadership that most people don't see until they're caught in it: The better you get at being indispensable, the more you prevent everyone around you from developing their own capability. Your team learns to wait for you. Your organization becomes brittle. And you become progressively more isolated because heroes don't admit uncertainty, ask for help, or show the kind of vulnerability that creates genuine connection.

"Let me tell you about *hygge*," I say, gesturing to the dumpling shop around us. "Most people think it's about candles and comfort, especially in high-pressure contexts. That's not it at all."

Wei leans forward, interested despite himself.

"*Hygge* is about the quality of presence. Being fully here, in this moment, with these people, doing this thing—whatever that thing is. You can have *hygge* in a crisis meeting if everyone is genuinely present with the problem. You can lack *hygge* at a family dinner if everyone is performing their roles rather than being with each other."

I pause to let this settle and pour more tea for both of us.

"This dumpling shop has *hygge*, even though it's humble and fluorescent-lit and serves food in twenty minutes or less. Because when you're here, you're *here*. The owner focuses on making dumplings well, not optimizing for scale. The customers eat slowly, tasting what's in front of them. Nobody is performing anything."

Wei nods slowly. "I've lost that completely. Somewhere between Copenhagen and Shanghai, between being a respected European operations director and becoming a Chinese CEO, I stopped being present and started performing constantly."

"And what's that performance costing you?"

"Everything that matters."

The Science Behind Hero-to-Human Leadership

Neuroscience of hero mode: Research from Stanford's Center for Compassion and Altruism Research shows that chronic hero leadership activates sustained cortisol response—the stress hormone associated with threat detection. When leaders operate from an "I must have all the answers" mindset, their brains remain in mild fight-or-flight mode, even during routine decisions.

This chronic activation impairs prefrontal cortex function—the brain region responsible for strategic thinking, emotional regulation, and complex decision-making. Studies tracking 400+ executives found that those scoring high on "hero leadership" metrics made 23% more strategic errors than those practicing vulnerable, distributed leadership.

The brain literally functions better when you admit uncertainty than when you pretend to have answers you don't have. Cognitive load decreases, strategic capacity increases.

Team development and learned helplessness: University of Michigan research on organizational behavior tracked 89 teams over three years, comparing "hero-led" teams (where the leader solves most problems) versus "distributed-authority" teams (where problems are solved closest to the work).

Results showed a predictable pattern:

- Year 1: Hero-led teams performed 15+% better (hero's expertise drove immediate results).
- Year 2: Distributed-authority teams caught up as capability developed.
- Year 3: Distributed teams outperformed hero-led teams by 31%.
- Hero-led teams showed classic learned helplessness: stopped problem-solving independently, waited for leader intervention even in routine situations.

Hero leadership creates short-term performance at the expense of long-term capability development. You're optimizing for today while undermining tomorrow.

Vulnerability and trust research: Contrary to common belief about vulnerability as weakness, Brené Brown's research (validated by multiple academic studies at Houston and Texas universities) shows that selective vulnerability enhances rather than undermines leadership authority.

Studies of 1,200+ leader-team relationships found:

- Leaders who admitted uncertainty had teams with 47% higher psychological safety scores.
- Teams with vulnerable leaders brought forward problems 38% earlier, preventing minor issues from becoming crises.
- Vulnerability from a position of strength (not seeking validation, just being honest) increased trust without decreasing respect.
- Teams led by vulnerable leaders showed 29% higher innovation rates.

Vulnerability isn't weakness—it's strategic honesty that enables distributed intelligence. The leader who says "I don't know" creates permission for collective problem-solving.

East–west leadership integration: IMD Business School research on cross-cultural leadership examined 300 executives who worked in both Asian and Western contexts over 5+ years and found that effective leaders integrated rather than chose between cultural approaches.

Key findings:

- "Hero mode" exists across all cultures but manifests with different characteristics.
- Sustainable leadership principles (presence, vulnerability, distributed authority) resonate across cultures when translated into local frameworks.
- Leaders who abandoned one cultural approach for another performed 19% worse than those who integrated both.
- Most effective leaders: 31% higher performance by finding universal human needs beneath cultural differences.

Cultural differences are fundamental in expression, but the hero-to-human shift isn't culturally specific. Every culture has concepts around presence, balance, and sustainable effectiveness—they just use different language.

Presence and leadership effectiveness: Mindfulness research from Harvard Medical School and Massachusetts General Hospital shows that leader presence (measured by attention quality, emotional regulation, and non-reactive decision-making) correlates strongly with effectiveness:

- 27% better strategic decision quality
- 34% higher team engagement
- 41% better crisis management outcomes
- 29% lower team burnout rates
- 23% faster problem resolution

Brain imaging studies show that leaders practicing presence show increased activity in the prefrontal cortex (executive function) and decreased activity in the amygdala (threat response), even under high stress conditions.

Presence isn't a soft skill—it's a cognitive capacity that enables better leadership. When you're fully present, your brain works better.

Long-term sustainability studies: Wharton School 15-year longitudinal research tracked 847 executive careers, comparing "hero leaders" (high intensity, low boundaries, indispensable positioning) versus "integrated leaders" (sustainable pace, distributed authority, human-centered approach).

Results over 15 years:

- Hero leaders: Higher initial success trajectory, 73% higher rate of serious health events (heart disease, severe burnout, substance issues), average senior leadership tenure 6.2 years before stepping back or breaking down
- Integrated leaders: Slower initial success, sustained over more extended periods, average tenure 11.8 years, 68% lower serious health issues, 34% higher long-term career earnings

Hero leadership is a sprint strategy in a marathon context. Integrated human leadership is sustainable over decades and ultimately more profitable both personally and professionally.

The Humanity Scale: A Framework for Integration

I pull out my notebook and start sketching the Humanity Scale. It's not a ladder you climb once, I explain to Wei. It's a map showing where you are under different conditions and a framework for recognizing when you've slipped back into hero mode.

"There are five stages," I tell him. "Most leaders move back and forth between them depending on stress levels, context, and whether they're conscious of the pattern. The goal isn't to reach Stage 5 and stay there forever. It's to develop the capacity to notice which stage you're in and consciously move toward integration."

Stage 1: The Indispensable Hero

I write this at the top of the page. Wei recognizes it immediately—his hand goes unconsciously to his chest, where the stress pain lives.

"This is where your identity is completely fused with being the person who solves everything," I explain. "Every problem feels like a test. Every decision you make personally feels like proof of value. Every all-nighter pulls feels like evidence of commitment."

"That's exactly it," Wei says. "I can't separate my worth from my usefulness. When I'm not solving problems, I feel purposeless."

"The belief driving this stage: 'My worth comes from being needed'. The team impact: They learn to be dependent. Why develop judgment when yours is always available? The sustainability: heading straight toward breakdown. You can run Stage 1 for a while on adrenaline and fear, but eventually the system collapses. Your chest pains, Lin's departure, Li's resignation—these aren't separate crises. They're the same crisis manifesting in different domains."

Wei is nodding as I speak, recognizing himself completely in this description.

Stage 2: The Reluctant Delegator

"This is the trap most hero leaders fall into when they realize Stage 1 is unsustainable," I continue. "You start delegating tasks but not decisions. Give people work to do, but hover over every choice. Ask for input but override it when it differs from your judgment."

"I've been there," Wei admits. "Multiple times. Each time I told myself I was 'developing my team' while just performing delegation without surrendering authority. Li saw through it immediately. She didn't need task delegation. She needed decision authority."

"Exactly. Stage 2 feels like progress because you're technically delegating, but it's micromanagement masquerading as mentorship. The belief: 'I'll let others help, but I need to supervise closely'. The team impact: People feel patronized rather than empowered. Resentment builds."

Stage 3: The Systems Builder

"This is where real transformation begins," I tell him. "You start recognizing that your job isn't to demonstrate your own capability—it's to build systems where others can develop theirs."

Wei's eyes light up. "That's what I did in Copenhagen. I built systems, documented decision frameworks, and created clarity about who owned what. Then, when problems arose, people had the authority and context to solve them. My job was architecting the system, not running every process within it."

"Exactly. The belief shifts to: 'My value comes from creating conditions for others to succeed'. The team impact: People start taking real ownership. They make decisions, encounter consequences, and learn from results. Some failures happen, but that's how capability develops."

I can see Wei doing the math in his head—calculating how far he's fallen from Stage 3 back to Stage 1 in his attempt to prove himself as a Chinese CEO.

Stage 4: The Vulnerable Leader

"Here's where it gets uncomfortable," I say. "Stage 4 requires admitting what you don't know, asking for help instead of only offering it, showing uncertainty without apologizing for it."

Wei visibly tenses. "In Chinese business culture, that looks like weakness. Admitting you don't know something feels like admitting you don't deserve your position."

"That's the false choice hero leadership creates," I counter. "But is the culture different, or is that your assumption? Because I've worked with Chinese leaders who practice vulnerability effectively. They just translate it appropriately—not as apologizing for ignorance, but as inviting collective intelligence."

Wei considers this. Around us, the lunch crowd is starting to arrive, the dumpling shop shifts from breakfast rhythm to midday efficiency.

"The belief at Stage 4: 'Vulnerability creates trust, and trust enables performance'," I continue. "The team impact: Psychological safety emerges. People bring you problems earlier because they're not afraid of judgment. They share concerns about your leadership because they trust you can hear them. Distributed intelligence happens."

Stage 5: The Integrated Human

"The final stage isn't about achieving permanent enlightenment," I explain. "It's about having a clear enough identity beyond your professional role that you can show up as a whole person who leads, rather than just a leader who happens to be human."

"What's the difference?" Wei asks.

"The belief: 'My presence matters more than my productivity'. The team impact: They operate at high levels whether you're present or not. They've developed independent capability because you built systems for it. They consult you for insight, not approval. The marker: Your team tells you 'we've got this' and you believe them."

I tap my notebook for emphasis. "Here's the critical thing: The stages aren't linear. Stress pushes you back toward hero mode. A crisis triggers your indispensable instincts. You don't graduate from the stages. You develop the capacity to notice when you've regressed and consciously return to integration."

Wei studies my sketch, recognizing himself scattered across multiple stages. With Li on operations: Stage 2 at best. With his finance team: maybe Stage 3. With Lin: not even on the scale—he's stopped showing up as human at all.

"The question isn't whether you're at Stage 5 consistently," I tell him. "It's whether you can recognize which stage you're in at any moment, and whether you have tools to move toward integration when you notice you've slipped."

Hero Leadership and Artificial Intelligence

"There's something else making this shift more urgent," I continue. "Something beyond personal sustainability or team effectiveness."

Wei looks up from the notebook, waiting.

"Artificial intelligence is making hero leadership obsolete. Not just unsustainable, but obsolete."

Wei frowns. "I'm not sure I follow."

"The hero leader's value proposition has always been: I know things others don't know. I can analyze situations faster. I can solve problems that stump my team. I'm indispensable because of my superior capability."

"Yes. That's exactly the belief."

"But AI can now know more than any human. It can analyze faster than any one human. It can generate solutions to problems that would have taken you days to work through. If your value as a leader comes from being the smartest person in the room, you're now competing with systems that never sleep, never tire, and have read more than you ever could."

Wei sits back, processing this. Around us, the dumpling shop continues to fill up, oblivious to the conversation about technological disruption happening over tea and pork dumplings.

"So what's left?" he asks. "If AI can do the hero work better than heroes, what's the point of human leadership?"

"That's exactly the right question. And the answer is: everything AI cannot do. Presence. Wisdom. Judgment developed through lived experience. The capacity to sit with uncertainty without rushing to resolution. The ability to build trust through vulnerability. The skill of reading a room in ways that go beyond data analysis."

I tap my sketch of the Humanity Scale. "Look at the stages. Stage 1, the Indispensable Hero, is increasingly a role that machines can play. They can have all the answers. They can solve all the problems. They can be available around the clock without burning out."

"But they can't move to Stage 5."

"Exactly. They can't be an Integrated Human because they're not human. They can't practice *hygge* because they can't be present. They can't build trust through vulnerability because they can't be vulnerable. They can't create the conditions for collective intelligence because they don't have relationships, they have interactions."

Wei is quiet for a moment, then laughs softly. "So, the technology that threatens to make leaders obsolete is forcing us to become more human, not less."

"That's the paradox. AI handles the transactional, the analytical, the problem-solving that used to define hero leadership. What remains valuable is precisely what you abandoned when you came back to China and started performing the role of hero CEO. The presence. The experience. The capacity to be fully human with the people you lead."

"Lin would appreciate the irony," Wei says. "I've been working harder than ever to prove my value, and the thing that would make me valuable is the thing I stopped doing: being present."

The Walk Through Two Worlds

We pay for breakfast and start walking.

We head toward the Bund, but take the long route through the French Concession, where tree-lined streets create a canopy over colonial-era buildings that Shanghai somehow preserved while demolishing everything else.

"Tell me about Copenhagen," I say. "Not the role, not the company. The life. What was different?"

Wei is quiet for a while, his pace slowing as memory pulls him back fifteen years.

"Morning bike rides to the office," he says finally. "Joining the river of other cyclists—executives, students, and delivery workers all sharing the same bike lanes. Team lunches that lasted fortyfive minutes where we talked about life, not just work. Friday bars at four o'clock, where you'd have a beer with colleagues and go home afterward, not back to your desk."

He pauses at a corner where modern Shanghai reasserts itself—glass towers reflecting afternoon light, cars honking with the special urgency that means nothing except that they can honk.

"Walking home through Christianshavn with Lin," he continues. "Stopping at the harbor to watch boats and making dinner together while listening to music and having conversations that weren't just logistics coordination. I was effective. Maybe more effective than I've ever been since. My team delivered consistently. We innovated. We hit targets. But I wasn't killing myself or anyone else to do it."

"And when you came back to China?"

"I convinced myself it wouldn't work here, different pressures, different culture, different expectations. I told myself Chinese companies needed different leadership—more intense, more hands-on, more heroic. The board hired me because of my European experience, but I abandoned it immediately to prove I was 'Chinese enough' for the role."

"And how's that working?" I ask, though the question is rhetorical at this point.

Wei laughs bitterly. "My wife is six thousand kilometers away, reconsidering our marriage. My best executive is leaving. My doctor thinks I'm a heart attack waiting to happen. And I'm leading a clean energy company—an industry literally built on sustainability principles—in the most unsustainable way imaginable."

We walk in silence for a while. The French Concession gives way to a business district—the sudden shift from human-scale to monumental that defines Shanghai's geographic split personality. Old plane trees and colonial villas on one side of the road, steel and glass towers reaching toward clouds on the other.

"What if," I say carefully, "the culture difference you perceived wasn't an actual difference? What if it was your fear of being seen as 'too European', and you responded by being an exaggerated version of what you thought Chinese leadership required?"

Wei stops walking. We're standing at the base of Shanghai Tower: 632 meters of vertical ambition that somehow hasn't fallen over despite being built on river mud and an earthquake zone. Around us, thousands of people move with purpose through the plaza—Chinese, European, American, a dozen nationalities all navigating the same space with their own internal logic.

"You're saying I created a false choice."

"I'm saying you abandoned what worked because you were afraid of appearing weak. But weakness isn't admitting you don't know everything. Weakness is pretending you do when everyone can see you don't."

Wei starts walking again, but slower now. Processing.

"The irony," he says after a while, "is that Chinese culture has concepts that align perfectly with what you're describing. 适意—*shìyì*—means a kind of ease and comfort that comes from alignment with natural rhythm. 中庸—*zhōngyōng*—is the middle way, avoiding extremes. These aren't foreign concepts. I just forgot them in my attempt to prove I was Chinese enough."

"Because you were performing Chineseness rather than being Chinese," I suggest.

"Yes. Exactly that."

Leader Spotlight: Nordic Leadership in Shanghai

Lars, a Danish CEO, was brought in to lead a Chinese solar technology company's expansion, with previous experience leading clean energy firms in Denmark and the UK. The board hired him specifically for his Nordic leadership approach—collaborative, sustainable, human-centered.

In the first six months, his vulnerability-based leadership style was perceived as a weakness by the Chinese management team. Direct reports waited for him to "act like a real CEO"—be decisive, have all answers, work around the clock. Several executives complained to the board that he wasn't "strong enough" for the role.

Instead of abandoning his approach, Lars doubled down with intention. He called an explicit team meeting where he addressed the elephant directly: "I was hired to bring Nordic leadership style to this organization. That means I won't pretend to have answers I don't have, I will protect sustainable pace, and I will distribute authority to those closest to the work. You can interpret this as weakness, or you can recognize it as a different form of strength. Your choice of which interpretation you select."

Lars studied the two Chinese concepts around balance (中庸—*zhōngyōng*) and ease (适意—*shìyì*) to help translate *hygge* and sustainable leadership into frameworks that resonated culturally (thanks Wei for teaching me). He started framing his approach using Chinese philosophical concepts: "Every culture has wisdom about presence and sustainability. I'm not importing Danish culture—I'm practicing universal principles that Danes happen to emphasize, and that Chinese tradition also honors."

Implementation over 18 months:

- Protected team lunches where work talk was limited to 20 minutes and the rest was relationship building
- Instituted "sustainable sprint" periods with explicit recovery built into project timelines
- Admitted uncertainties publicly, asked for team input on strategy before making decisions
- Went home at 6 p.m. consistently, never apologized for it, and made it clear this was the company norm
- Created decision frameworks so the team could act without his constant approval
- Established "red folder" system: Only truly urgent issues needed his immediate attention

Results:

- Employee retention improved 34% (industry average is 45% annual turnover in tech)
- Leadership team burnout incidents dropped from 5 per year to zero

- Promoted three internal candidates to the director level (previously only hired externally for senior roles)
- The company hit aggressive growth targets while the team worked 11–14% fewer hours than the industry average
- Employee engagement scores: 4.6/5 (up from 3.1/5 when he started)
- Productivity per employee increased 23%

Lars reflected: "They thought I was weak at first. Then they realized I was building something stronger—a team that could function without me constantly intervening. That's not weak leadership. That's strategic architecture. The hero CEO makes themselves indispensable. The human CEO makes themselves unnecessary for daily operations so they can focus on what requires CEO-level thinking."

Cultural differences are fundamental, but human needs for autonomy, growth, and sustainable pace are universal. The question isn't whether vulnerability-based leadership can work in different cultures—it's whether leaders dare to practice it consistently until trust develops. Lars succeeded not by being less Danish but by being more intentionally human in ways that transcended cultural categories.

Hygge as Presence, Not Performance

That evening, I got a message from Wei: "I'm at the dumpling shop again :). Lin is on a video call from Copenhagen. First real conversation we've had in months. Thought you should know."

I don't respond—he doesn't need my input. He needs to figure this out himself. But I'm pleased he recognized the significance of "our" location. Going back to that place, being present in it rather than performing through it—that's the practice.

Three days later, we meet for coffee. Wei looks different—not rested exactly, but more solid. Less fragmented.

"I told Lin about my new understanding of *hygge*," he says. "The real version, not the Instagram version. About the quality of presence. About being fully here rather than performing. She cried, which I wasn't expecting."

"Why did she cry?"

"Because she said that's the version of me she married. The one who could sit over dinner for three hours in Copenhagen and be nowhere else. The one who listened when she talked about her work instead of half-listening while thinking about his own. The one who took bike rides with her just for the sake of riding, not to optimize cardio or clear his head for the next meeting."

"And what did you tell her?"

"That I forgot how to do that. That somewhere between being a European-trained leader and a Chinese CEO, I lost the capacity for presence. Everything became a performance. Even our video calls felt like I was performing the role of attentive husband rather than being attentive."

I pour more coffee from the press between us. The café is crowded with afternoon workers, but our corner feels separate somehow. Protected.

"*Hygge* isn't about slowing down or opting out," I remind him. "You can have intense, high stakes work and still practice *hygge* if you're fully present with what you're doing. The opposite isn't rest—it's performance. When you're performing, you're always split. Part of you doing the thing, part of you monitoring how you're doing the thing, part of you managing what others think about how you're doing the thing."

"That's exhausting just to describe," Wei says.

"That's because it's exhausting to live. Hero mode is performance mode. You're never just doing your job—you're always proving you deserve to have the job. That fragmentation is what destroys *tilfredshed*—that deep Danish satisfaction that comes from alignment, not achievement."

Wei nods slowly. "Lin asked me what I'm going to do differently. I told her I didn't have a complete plan, but I was starting with presence. Being fully where I am instead of always being somewhere else in my head."

"That's not a small thing," I tell him. "That's the foundation everything else builds on."

The First Vulnerable Moment

A week later, Wei calls me from his office. "I'm about to do something that feels either brave or stupid. Can't tell which."

"What is it?"

"Executive team meeting in fifteen minutes. I'm going to tell them the truth. About why I've been micromanaging everything. About the fear driving it. About the gap between the leader they hired and the hero I've been performing."

"That's brave," I tell him. "Do you want to rehearse?"

"No. If I rehearse, it becomes a performance. I just need to show up and be honest."

"Then do that. Call me after if you need to process."

He calls back two hours later. I can hear something different in his voice—not relief exactly, but release.

"I started by telling them I've been failing them," he says. "Not just Li, though her resignation was the most visible symptom. All of them. That I've been operating from the belief that my value as CEO comes from having all the answers, solving all the problems, and being indispensable to every decision. That this belief has created a team that waits for me instead of leading."

"How did they respond?"

"Silence at first. That uncomfortable silence where everyone is recalculating what they thought they knew. Then Chen, my CFO, spoke up. Said they hired me because of my European experience. My ability to build high-performing teams without burning them out. My systems thinking. That they didn't hire me to become someone else."

I can picture the room, the tension of this moment.

"Then our head of R&D added that he has two PhDs and fifteen years of battery technology experience, but he's been waiting for my approval on experiments he's more qualified to design. Not because I demanded it—because I made myself available for everything, and he stopped trusting his own judgment."

"And Li?"

"Li said (in private after) she'll withdraw her resignation on one condition: I let her run operations. No more 'checking in' on decisions she's hired to make. No more swooping in to solve problems before she can learn from them. She needs me to be CEO, not super-COO."

"That's a clear boundary."

"I said yes immediately. And then I told them all I need help holding myself accountable. That's when I slip back into hero mode—and I will—I need them to call it out."

"That's vulnerable leadership," I tell him. "Stage 4 on the Humanity Scale. How do you feel?"

"Terrified," he admits. "But also, lighter. Like I've been carrying weight I didn't need to carry, and I can finally put it down."

Three Months of Practice

Wei and I meet monthly over the next three months. The transformation isn't dramatic or sudden—it's incremental and sometimes frustrating. He slips back into hero mode regularly, especially when stress spikes or crises emerge. But he catches himself faster each time.

In our October meeting, the changes are more evident. Lin has returned to Shanghai—not because everything is fixed, but because Wei is practicing what he said he would practice. They're in couples therapy twice a month, sessions he protects.

"Last week I almost took over a hiring decision from my head of operations," he tells me over virtual tea. "Caught myself mid-email, deleted what I'd written, sent a different message: 'What's your recommendation?' instead of 'Here's what I think you should do'."

"That's it," I tell him. "Noticing the pattern and choosing differently."

"It's hard. The instinct is so strong. I see a problem; I want to solve the problem. Brain tells me: this is your job, this is your value, this is why they pay you."

"But you're learning to distinguish between 'this is my job' and 'this is work I need to do personally'."

"Yes. And the company is functioning better. Li closed a €47 million contract with a German automotive company last week. I was helpful in the early stages, but she led the negotiation. R&D made a breakthrough on battery efficiency—I found out after it happened, not because I was hovering over the process. Chen restructured our financing in ways I wouldn't have thought of."

He pauses, pours more tea.

"Employee engagement scores are up 34%. Voluntary turnover is down to 7% from 19%. Board feedback is that company performance improved since I stopped being indispensable."

"And you?" I ask. "How are you?"

"Sleeping six hours consistently, which feels like luxury. Blood pressure is improving. Lin and I are rebuilding. I bike to work most days now, as I used to in Copenhagen. Sometimes I stop at a café and just sit for twenty minutes before going in."

"*Hygge*," I say.

"*Hygge*," he agrees. "It translates perfectly to Shanghai. It's not about geography or culture. It's about presence versus performance. About being human instead of being a hero."

I think about my own journey—the years I spent performing invincibility while fragmenting internally, the marriages I damaged by never being present, the teams I kept dependent because their dependence confirmed my value. Wei's learning in months what took me years to understand.

"What would you tell yourself eighteen months ago?" I ask him. "The version taking the CEO role convinced him that he needed to be indispensable?"

Wei considers this carefully. Around us, the café has its late afternoon rhythm—students with laptops, businesspeople having meetings, the energy of a city that never quite stops moving.

"I'd tell him that sustainable leadership builds sustainable companies. That vulnerability isn't the opposite of strength—it's the foundation of it. That the team doesn't need you to have all the answers, they need you to create conditions where they can find answers collectively."

He rotates his teacup, a gesture I've noticed he does when thinking deeply.

"I'd tell him that his marriage is more important than his quarterly targets. That presence is more valuable than productivity. That the leadership approach he learned in Europe wasn't wrong—abandoning it was wrong."

"And the hero leadership?"

"I'd tell him it's a trap. It feels like strength, looks like commitment, and gets rewarded with promotions and respect. But it's a sophisticated form of self-destruction. You burn yourself out while preventing others from developing capability. And the antidote isn't working less or caring less. It's being fully present in what you're doing instead of constantly performing for an imagined audience."

This understanding didn't come cheap. It cost Wei his sense of security, temporarily his marriage, and nearly his health. But he's integrating now in ways that will serve him for decades. The hero was impressive and exhausting and fragile. The human is present, collaborative, and resilient.

"One more thing," Wei adds. "I'd tell him that stepping down from hero to human isn't stepping down. It's stepping into something more sustainable and ultimately more effective. Same role, completely different approach. And far more satisfying—not achievement satisfaction, but that deeper *tilfredshed* that comes from alignment between who you are and what you do."

What I Wish I'd Known: The Cost of Being Indispensable

The cost of being indispensable to my career was becoming disposable to my relationships. My worth came from solving every problem, having every answer, and being needed by everyone. What I was doing was preventing my team from developing capability while destroying my capacity for genuine connection with the people I loved.

When I finally learned to say, "I don't know" and "I need help," I expected my authority to diminish. It didn't. It distributed. My team didn't respect me less—they trusted me more. Because vulnerability doesn't undermine leadership. Pretending you don't need anything from anyone undermines leadership.

The hardest lesson: The leadership approaches that work in one context don't need to be abandoned in another. You can integrate rather than choose. I spent years thinking I needed to be one kind of leader or another—Danish or American, collaborative or heroic, vulnerable or strong. The actual wisdom was recognizing these aren't opposites. The best leadership integrates across apparent contradictions.

My partners didn't need me to be a hero. They required me to be present. My teams didn't need me to have all the answers. They required me to create conditions where they could find answers collectively. My companies didn't need me to be indispensable. They needed me to build systems that worked without requiring my constant intervention.

Hygge isn't Danish. It's human. It's about the quality of presence in whatever you're doing. And hero mode destroys presence because you're always performing rather than being. The relief I felt when I stopped performing and started being present—that's available to anyone willing to step down from hero to human.

It's not actually stepping down. It's stepping into your full humanity, which is the only foundation sustainable enough to support long-term effectiveness.

The Hero-to-Human Four-Week Practice

Moving from hero to human leadership requires systematic practice. Here's a four-week structure that builds capacity incrementally.

Week 1: Recognition and Awareness

Daily Practice (15 minutes):

- **Morning:** Set an intention to notice when you're in hero mode versus human mode throughout the day.
- **Evening:** Journal three moments—one where you were genuinely present, one where you performed competence, one where you defaulted to solving instead of enabling.

Weekly Practice (60 minutes):

- **Map your hero patterns:** When do you most strongly feel the need to be indispensable? What triggers it?
- **Track your interventions:** For one whole week, note every time you solve a problem someone else could solve.
- **Reflection question:** "What would happen if I didn't rescue this situation?"

Success Metric: You can articulate your specific hero triggers and identify at least three situations this week where you solved something someone else could have figured out.

Week 2: Small Experiments in Stepping Back

Daily Practice (20 minutes):

- **Morning:** Identify one meeting or decision where you'll ask questions instead of providing answers.
- **Afternoon:** Practice saying, "I don't know, what do you think?" at least once.
- **Evening:** Notice your discomfort with not having or sharing the answer.

Weekly Practice (90 minutes):

- **Delegate one significant decision completely:** Brief the person, give them authority, don't rescue if they struggle.
- **Document your anxiety:** What are you afraid will happen if you don't intervene?
- **Reality check:** Did your worst fears materialize when you stepped back?

Success Metric: You've enabled at least one team decision without your intervention and observed that the sky didn't fall.

Week 3: Strategic Vulnerability

Daily Practice (25 minutes):

- **Morning:** Share one genuine uncertainty with your team (not fake vulnerability, real "I don't know").
- **Midday:** Ask for help on something instead of figuring it out alone.
- **Evening:** Reflect on whether admitting uncertainty diminished or enhanced your authority.

Weekly Practice (2 hours):

- **Have one vulnerable conversation with someone on your team:** Share something you're genuinely struggling with.
- **Ask explicitly:** "What do you need from me to lead effectively in your domain?"
- **Listen** without defending, explaining, or immediately solving.

Success Metric: You've demonstrated genuine vulnerability at least three times without your authority collapsing and possibly seeing trust increase.

Week 4: Presence over Performance

Daily Practice (30 minutes):

- **Morning:** One interaction where you're fully present, not performing competence.
- **Midday:** Practice complete presence in whatever you're doing, even if it's intense.
- **Evening:** Audit your day: Where were you performing versus being?

Weekly Practice (3 hours):

- **Identify one relationship where you've been in hero mode:** with your partner, your team, your board.
- **Have a conversation** about what they need versus what you've been providing.
- **Design one significant boundary** that supports your presence (e.g., "no work after 7 p.m.," "Tuesdays protected for strategic thinking").

Success Metric: You've established at least one boundary that protects your capacity for presence and begun noticing the difference between performing and being.

Ongoing Integration

After four weeks, assess which stage of the Humanity Scale you're operating from in different contexts. The work isn't to reach Stage 5 everywhere all the time—it's to develop the capacity to notice when you've slipped into hero mode and consciously return to human mode.

Use the scale diagnostically:

- When you feel overwhelmed: Which stage am I in?
- When your team seems dependent: What am I doing that reinforces their dependency?
- When you're exhausted despite "success": Am I performing or being present?

The goal isn't perfection. It's integration—bringing your full humanity to your leadership rather than fragmenting into hero performance.

Questions for Reflection

Transformational Question: Who are you afraid of becoming if you stop being the hero?

Personal Awareness: When do you most strongly feel the need to be the hero? What are you afraid will happen if you step into human mode instead? What relationships are you sacrificing to maintain your hero identity? Where does your sense of worth come from—being needed or being effective?

Systemic Thinking: Have you absorbed leadership approaches from different contexts that you're now abandoning? What worked before that have you stopped doing? If you're performing a version of leadership to prove something, who are you trying to convince? How has your hero mode trained your team to be dependent rather than capable?

Action-Oriented: What's one decision this week that you could step back from entirely? Who could you trust to figure it out without your intervention? What would you need to admit to your team to enable their independence? What boundary would support your presence rather than your performance?

Integration: Where in your life outside work do you also perform hero mode? What has your partner or family sacrificed for your hero performance? What would it feel like to be fully human—uncertain, vulnerable, present—in your most important relationships? When was the last time you experienced complete presence without performance?

From Indispensable to Integrated

I'm in my Copenhagen apartment when Wei sends me a message six months after our first dumpling shop conversation. It's a photo: Lin and he are on bikes along Shanghai's Huangpu River, both smiling in that unselfconscious way that happens when you're not posing for the camera, just being captured in a moment of genuine presence.

The text reads: "We rode for two hours this morning. Just riding. No optimization, no agenda. Li sent an update while we were out—closed another major contract, didn't need my input. The company is thriving. Marriage is rebuilding. I'm sleeping seven hours now. Still slip into hero mode sometimes but catch it faster. *Hygge* works in Shanghai the same as in Copenhagen. Just took me 18 months and almost losing everything to remember. Thank you."

I don't respond immediately. Some messages don't need responses. They just need to be received.

Later, I think about the leaders I've worked with who made this shift—from hero to human, from performance to presence, from indispensable to integrated. None of them regretted it. Many of them said it saved their lives, their marriages, their health, their companies. All of them said it was more complicated than they expected and more worthwhile than they imagined.

The framework gives you the model—five stages from indispensable hero to integrated human. The practices give you the tools—four weeks of systematic capacity building. The research confirms what experience teaches—hero mode destroys what it claims to protect.

But integration only happens when you're willing to be uncertain, vulnerable, and fully present. When you stop performing strength and start practicing humanity. When you recognize that the team doesn't need you to have all the answers, they need you to create conditions where collective intelligence can emerge.

That's not a weakness. That's the foundation of sustainable leadership.

Being human means having the conversations you've been avoiding—the ones where you don't have answers, where you can't control outcomes, where all you have is your honest presence. And those conversations, as Wei was learning in therapy and executive meetings and bike rides with Lin, were the real test of whether humanity was performance or practice.

The framework reveals what wholeness requires. But integration happens only when you stop trying to be the hero and start being human. That's the shift we explore in the conversations that matter most—the difficult ones where vulnerability meets truth. And that territory is waiting for us in Chapter 10.

10 The Conversations That Matter

Why the words we avoid speaking shape the lives we end up living.

The freight elevator groans its way to the fourth floor, cables straining against decades of use. Through the metal grate, I watch each level pass: ground-floor warehouses now converted to galleries, second-floor architecture firms with their vast drawing tables visible through industrial windows, third-floor photography studios where someone has left the lights on overnight. The building smells of old timber and fresh espresso, a Vienna combination of history refusing to be entirely modern.

Katharina's creative agency occupies the entire fourth floor of this converted factory in Neubau, Vienna's seventh district. The neighborhood is the creative reinvention that certain cities do well: former industrial spaces now housing design studios, recording facilities, and the kind of advertising agencies that win awards at Cannes but still feel like scrappy startups.

The elevator door slides open with a metallic screech, and I step into a space that tells you everything about its founder before you meet her. Exposed brick walls covered with campaign mockups and typography experiments. Mismatched furniture that somehow coheres into an aesthetic.

A vintage jukebox in the corner that I later learn works. Enormous windows letting in the gray morning, the kind of light that photographers love because it flatters everything equally.

A young man with an elaborate tattoo sleeve and impeccable posture looks up from a standing desk. "You must be Peter. Katharina said to send you straight through. She's in there." He gestures toward a glass-walled conference space where someone is pacing, phone pressed to ear, free hand cutting the air with determined emphasis.

I wait outside the glass, watching her work. Katharina is forty-four, though she moves with the restless energy of someone younger. Her silver-streaked dark hair is pulled back in a way that suggests efficiency rather than style, and she wears the kind of simple black clothing that creative directors favor because it disappears, letting the work be the only thing with color. Through the glass, I can hear fragments: ". . . not what we agreed . . ." and ". . . the timeline was clear . . ." and finally, ". . . we need to discuss this in person."

She ends the call and stands motionless for a moment, staring at nothing. Then something shifts in her posture, a visible reassembly, and she opens the glass door with a smile that almost reaches her eyes.

"Peter. Thank you for coming all this way. Coffee? We have an Italian machine that costs more than my first car." She leads me to a small kitchen alcove where the espresso machine, which indeed looks like a small car, too. "I should warn you, I'm not entirely sure why I reached out. I just know something needs to change, and I've run out of ideas for what. And how."

The Weight of Unspoken Words

Over the next hour, Katharina's story emerges in fragments, like pieces of a puzzle she's not sure how to assemble.

The agency she built from nothing fifteen years ago now employs forty-seven people across Vienna, London, and a small satellite office in Milan. They've won industry recognition, attracted premium clients, and built a reputation for work that is both commercially effective and creatively ambitious. By any external measure, Katharina has succeeded.

"I feel like I'm running a theater production," she tells me, both hands wrapped around her espresso cup as though drawing warmth from it. "Every day, I perform the role of confident creative director. I say the things a leader should say. I make the decisions a founder should make. And at night I go home to an apartment that's beautiful and empty, and I wonder when my life became something I watch rather than something I live."

The particulars vary, but I've heard versions of this story from leaders across industries and continents. The successful exterior hides an interior that feels increasingly hollow. The performance of confidence masking genuine uncertainty. The growing gap between the life others see and the life being lived.

"What conversations are you avoiding?" I ask because experience has taught me that this question often reveals more than hours of discussion about strategy or structure.

Katharina sets down her cup, and something flickers across her face. Recognition, perhaps. Or fear.

"My business partner, Lukas. We founded this agency together, but we haven't agreed on a direction in three years. Every strategic meeting becomes a dance around a consensus that neither of us believes. We smile and nod and then do whatever we were going to do anyway."

She pauses, looks out the window at the Vienna rooftops.

"My creative director, Marta. She's brilliant, but she's also burning out, and I can see it happening, and I haven't said anything because I don't know what to offer her. So I pretend I don't notice, and she pretends she's fine, and we both know we're pretending."

Another pause, longer this time.

"My mother. She's seventy-eight, and she keeps asking when I'm going to stop working so much and find someone. And instead of telling her that I'm lonely too, that I want connection, but I don't know how to make space for it anymore, I change the subject. Every time. For years now."

She turns back to face me. "The list keeps going. But you're not asking for an inventory, are you?"

"No," I say. "I'm asking because the conversations we avoid don't disappear. They accumulate. And eventually, they become the architecture of our lives."

The Coherence We Crave

In Danish, we have a word that captures something essential about what Katharina was experiencing: *sammenhæng*. It translates roughly as "coherence" or "connection," but it means something more profound.

Sammenhæng is the sense that all parts of your life fit together, that there's a through-line connecting who you are at work and who you are at home and who you are with friends and who you are alone with your thoughts.

When sammenhæng is present, life feels integrated and decisions in one domain support rather than undermine decisions in others. Your professional values align with your personal ones. The self you present to the world resembles the self you experience internally.

When sammenhæng is absent, life feels fragmented. You become different people in different contexts, and the energy required to maintain these separate selves becomes exhausting. You start to feel like an actor who has forgotten which role is yours.

Here's what I've learned from working with leaders like Katharina: The conversations we avoid are the primary destroyers of sammenhæng. Every unspoken truth creates a minor fracture between who we are and who we present ourselves to be. Over time, these fractures accumulate until we no longer recognize the life we're living as our own.

Katharina's avoidance of conversation with Lukas wasn't just a business problem. It was eroding her sense of integrity. Every meeting where she feigned consensus, she didn't feel was a meeting where she practiced being someone other than herself. Every strategic decision made without genuine alignment was a brick in the wall between her authentic self and her professional identity.

Her silence with Marta wasn't just a management failure. It was a betrayal of the kind of leader she wanted to be. Every day she watched someone struggle without offering support was a day she accumulated evidence against her own values.

Her deflection with her mother wasn't just family awkwardness. It was a missed opportunity for the very connection she longed for. Every changed subject was a door closed against intimacy.

The pattern was clear: Katharina was trading short-term comfort for long-term fragmentation. And she'd been making that trade so long, she'd forgotten it was a choice.

The Anatomy of Avoidance

Understanding why we avoid difficult conversations requires understanding what we're really protecting. On the surface, it seems obvious: We avoid hard conversations because they're uncomfortable. But that explanation is incomplete. Discomfort is temporary. The consequences of avoidance are often permanent.

Avoidance as Protection

What I've discovered through my own experience and my work with hundreds of leaders is that we typically avoid difficult conversations to protect one of four things:

- **Identity Protection.** We avoid conversations that might challenge how we see ourselves. Katharina avoided talking with Lukas because doing so would require admitting that the partnership wasn't working, which would mean acknowledging that something she'd helped create was flawed. Her identity as a successful founder was tangled up with the success of that relationship.
- **Relationship Preservation.** We avoid conversations we fear might damage essential relationships. Katharina didn't confront Marta's burnout because she was afraid the conversation might lead somewhere neither of them wanted to go. Better to maintain the fiction of "everything is fine" than risk the relationship changing.
- **Outcome Uncertainty.** We avoid conversations when we don't know what we want the outcome to be. Katharina didn't engage with her mother's questions about loneliness because she didn't have an answer. She couldn't fix her own situation, so she couldn't bear to name it.
- **Competence Maintenance.** We avoid conversations that might reveal we don't have all the answers. Leaders like Katharina often feel pressure to appear in control. Admitting uncertainty, asking for input, or acknowledging struggle can feel like professional suicide.

The tragedy is that these protective strategies usually produce the outcomes they're meant to prevent. Avoiding the conversation with Lukas didn't protect their partnership; it hollowed it out. Not addressing Marta's burnout didn't preserve their relationship; it guaranteed Marta would eventually leave. Deflecting her mother's questions didn't protect Katharina from the pain of loneliness; it ensured she would face that loneliness without support.

We build elaborate architectures of avoidance, thinking we're constructing shelters. What we're building are prisons.

Technology as a Trap

These architectures of avoidance have become more sophisticated in recent years. Artificial intelligence offers new ways to avoid the conversations that matter while appearing to communicate effectively.

You can have AI draft the difficult email instead of having the difficult conversation. You can use AI to craft the perfect message, calibrated for tone and diplomacy, while never sitting with another person in the discomfort of genuine dialogue. You can delegate the words while avoiding the encounter.

I've watched leaders use these tools with increasing sophistication. One executive I worked with had AI draft every sensitive communication: performance feedback, strategic disagreements, even the message telling his business partner they needed to discuss the future of their relationship. The messages were technically excellent. Clear, professional, emotionally intelligent in structure if not in origin.

"I'm communicating more than ever," he told me. "I send thoughtful messages on every difficult topic." All proud.

"But when was the last time you had a difficult conversation?" I asked. "Not sent a message about a difficult topic. Actually sat with someone in the discomfort of saying something hard and hearing their response in real time."

He couldn't really remember.

This is the trap: AI can help you communicate about difficult things, but it cannot help you have the conversation. It can draft the words, but it cannot be present for the response. It can optimize your message, but it cannot create *sammenhæng*, that Danish sense of coherence and connection that only emerges when two people are genuinely present with each other.

The conversations that matter cannot be delegated. They cannot be optimized. They cannot be mediated through technology that protects you from the vulnerability of genuine encounter. The whole point of a difficult conversation is the difficulty itself, the willingness to be uncomfortable together, to not know how it will go, to risk the relationship to deepen it.

AI makes it easier than ever to avoid this work while feeling like you're doing it. You can send more messages, craft better communications, manage more relationships at a distance. But the conversations that matter, the ones that heal ruptures and build trust and create genuine connection, those still require what they've always required: Two humans, present with each other, willing to be uncomfortable together.

Katharina had been using technology as one of her avoidance strategies. She communicated constantly with Lukas through email and Slack, but they hadn't had an actual conversation about their partnership in months. The volume of communication was masking the absence of connection.

The Difficult Conversations Framework

Over the past five years, I've developed a systematic approach to the conversations that matter most. It's not about scripts or techniques for manipulation. It's about creating conditions where truth can emerge without destroying connection.

The framework has four elements that work together.

Element One: Name the Gap

Most difficult conversations become difficult because we're talking around the real issue rather than naming it directly. The first step is identifying and articulating the gap between what is and what should be, between what's being said and what's being felt, between the current reality and the desired future.

For Katharina and Lukas, the gap wasn't about strategy. It was about trust. They no longer trusted each other's judgment, and every strategic disagreement was really a proxy war for that more profound rupture.

Naming the gap requires courage because it often means saying something that hasn't been said before. But it's also a relief because it ends the exhausting performance of pretending the gap doesn't exist.

Element Two: Own Your Part

Difficult conversations almost always involve mutual contribution to the problem. We want to believe we're innocent victims of others' behavior, but that's rarely the complete picture. Owning your part isn't about accepting blame or letting others off the hook. It's about demonstrating the vulnerability that makes genuine dialogue possible.

When Katharina eventually had the conversation with Lukas, she started by acknowledging her own role in their dysfunction. She'd been avoiding conflict, making unilateral decisions, and building her own power base within the agency rather than working to strengthen their partnership. This wasn't a weakness. It was the foundation for a conversation between equals rather than opponents.

Element Three: Seek Understanding Before Agreement

The goal of a difficult conversation isn't to win. It's to understand and be understood. This requires genuine curiosity about the other person's perspective, even when that perspective seems wrong or unreasonable.

Most of us enter difficult conversations with our arguments fully formed, waiting for the other person to stop talking so we can deploy them. This isn't dialogue. It's a competitive monologue. Real understanding requires setting aside your position long enough to explore theirs genuinely.

Katharina discovered that Lukas wasn't trying to undermine her. He was afraid. Afraid the agency had grown beyond what he could manage, afraid his creative skills were becoming obsolete, afraid she would eventually push him out. His defensive behavior was a protection against fears he'd never articulated because she'd never asked.

Element Four: Create New Commitments

Understanding is necessary but not sufficient. Difficult conversations need to end with clear commitments about what will be different going forward. Without new commitments, even the most profound conversation becomes just another instance of talking without changing.

These commitments should be specific, time-bound, and mutually held. Not "we'll communicate better" but "we'll have a one-hour strategic alignment meeting every Monday, with no phones, where we'll discuss one decision we need to make together." Not "I'll be more supportive" but "I'll ask you three genuine questions about your experience before I offer any advice."

New commitments transform conversations from events into processes. They create accountability structures that extend the conversation's impact beyond the moment of speaking.

The Science Behind Authentic Conversation

The research on avoided conversations extends beyond common sense into measurable physiological and psychological effects. What we don't say shapes more than relationships; it shapes our health.

- **Suppression and Health.** Research from the University of Texas demonstrates that actively suppressing thoughts and emotions requires significant cognitive resources and correlates with increased stress hormones, compromised immune function, and higher rates of cardiovascular issues. The effort of not saying something is physiologically costly.
- **Authenticity and Well-Being.** Studies from the University of Virginia found that people who report being able to express their authentic selves in their primary relationships show significantly lower rates of depression and anxiety. The gap between internal experience and external expression is itself a source of psychological distress.
- **Organizational Impact.** Harvard Business School research on psychological safety shows that teams where members feel safe to express concerns, disagree openly, and raise complex issues outperform teams where such conversations are avoided. The correlation holds across industries and cultures.
- **The Zeigarnik Effect.** Psychological research demonstrates that uncompleted tasks occupy more mental space than completed ones. Avoided conversations function similarly. They create open loops that consume cognitive resources even when we're not consciously thinking about them.
- **Relational Quality.** Gottman Institute research on relationship longevity shows that the ability to have difficult conversations productively is one of the strongest predictors of relationship survival. Couples who avoid conflict don't have better relationships; they have relationships that are more likely to end.

Avoiding difficult conversations is not a neutral act of self-protection. It's an active choice that carries measurable costs to health, well-being, relationships, and effectiveness.

Cross-Cultural Variations in Difficult Conversations

The way different cultures approach difficult conversations reveals much about what those cultures value and fear. Understanding these variations can help us develop more flexible approaches to the conversations that matter.

- **The Direct Approach (Northern European).** Danish, Dutch, and German cultures tend to appreciate directness in communication. Difficult conversations are approached as problems to be solved through clear articulation of positions and logical discussion of options. The strength of this approach is efficiency and clarity. The weakness can be insufficient attention to emotional dimensions and relationship preservation.

  Katharina, despite being Austrian, had absorbed much of this Northern European directness through her work with German and Dutch clients. Her instinct was to approach difficult conversations as logical problems. This worked well for certain kinds of issues but left her unprepared for conversations where emotion and relationship were primary.
- **The Contextual Approach (Asian).** Many Asian cultures emphasize indirect communication and attention to context, relationship, and face-saving. Difficult messages are often conveyed through implication rather than explicit statement. The strength of this approach is the preservation of relationships and social harmony. The weakness can be ambiguity that allows problems to persist unaddressed.

  I worked with a Singaporean executive who explained it this way: "In my culture, saying 'that's an interesting approach' often means 'I completely disagree'. The message is there, but you have to listen differently to hear it." This indirectness isn't evasion. It's a different grammar of truth-telling, one that requires reading between lines rather than taking statements at face value.

- **The Relational Approach (Southern European and Latin American).** Italian, Spanish, and Latin American cultures often prioritize relationship warmth even in difficult conversations. Confrontation may be preceded by extensive relationship-building and followed by explicit efforts at reconciliation. The strength is the maintained connection. The weakness can be difficulty addressing issues that require clear boundaries.

  A peer in Rome once told me, "We can have the most difficult conversation imaginable, but we will do it over a long lunch, with good wine, and by the end, we will still be friends. The conversation and the relationship are separate things." This capacity to hold difficult content within warm relational containers is something Northern Europeans often struggle to replicate.
- **The Procedural Approach (American Corporate).** American business culture often approaches difficult conversations through process: performance reviews, feedback frameworks, and HR protocols. The strength is structure and documentation. The weakness can be a depersonalization that makes conversations feel like bureaucratic exercises rather than genuine human exchanges.

  I've watched American executives deliver devastating feedback with clinical precision, following the script perfectly while missing the human being across the table entirely. The input is technically excellent. But the person receiving it feels processed rather than addressed.

None of these approaches is inherently superior. The most effective communicators develop fluency across multiple styles, adapting their approach to the specific relationship, cultural context, and nature of the issue at hand. Sammenhæng doesn't require one style of communication. It requires authentic communication that bridges the gap between internal experience and external expression, whatever form that takes.

Leader Spotlight: The Cost of One Avoided Conversation

Marco ran a successful manufacturing company in northern Italy for twenty-three years. When I met him, he was dealing with the aftermath of "the conversation I should have had a decade ago."

His son, Alessandro, had joined the family business after university, and Marco had groomed him as the obvious successor. There was just one problem: Alessandro didn't want the job. He'd never liked it. But the conversation about alternative futures had never happened because Marco assumed desire was inherited along with capability, and Alessandro couldn't bear to disappoint his father.

For ten years, they both performed roles neither had chosen. Alessandro grew increasingly depressed; his work was adequate but joyless. Marco interpreted his son's lack of enthusiasm as insufficient dedication, responded with criticism, and widened the gap between them. The business suffered from leadership that was technically competent but emotionally vacant.

The truth finally emerged during a health crisis. Alessandro, hospitalized for stress-related chest pains at thirty-four, finally told his father: "I don't want your company. I never did. I wanted your approval, and I thought this was the only way to get it."

Marco was devastated—not by his son's confession, but by the decade of suffering that one avoided conversation had caused. "I would have been disappointed for a week," he told me. "Instead, I lost ten years of knowing my son. We were both pretending to have a relationship while having a business arrangement."

Today, Alessandro runs a small architectural firm and is, by his own account, genuinely happy for the first time in his adult life. Marco sold the manufacturing company to a competitor and now mentors young entrepreneurs. Their relationship, freed from the weight of unspoken expectations, has become something real. The conversation they finally had didn't destroy anything. It revealed that what they thought they were protecting had already been lost.

Finally Having Those Difficult Conversations

Over the following months, Katharina systematically worked through her list of avoided conversations. Not all at once. Not perfectly. But intentionally, with the framework as a guide.

The Partnership Conversation

The conversation with Lukas happened first, because it was the most urgent. The agency couldn't continue with two leaders pulling in different directions. They met outside the office, at a bar in the first district, where neither of them had professional associations, neutral territory for a conversation that needed space.

"I prepared for that conversation more than I've prepared for anything, really," Katharina shared. "I wrote out what I wanted to say. I practiced in front of a mirror, which felt ridiculous. I imagined every possible response he might have and how I would handle it. And then the actual conversation went nowhere as I'd planned, which is maybe the most important lesson."

"I started by naming what we'd both been avoiding. I said, 'I think we've lost trust in each other, and I think we've both been pretending that's not true'. The relief on his face was immediate. Like I'd said, something that had been pressing on both of us for years."

The conversation lasted three hours. It was uncomfortable. There were moments of defensiveness on both sides, accusations that stung, histories recounted differently. But by the end, they had a clearer picture of what had gone wrong and a set of specific commitments for what would be different.

The result wasn't a restored partnership. It was something more honest: a recognition that they wanted different things for the agency and needed to find a way to separate what they'd built together. Lukas would take the Berlin office, which had always been more his vision. Katharina would retain Vienna and London. The divorce was difficult but dignified. More importantly, it was real.

"I thought the conversation would destroy us," Katharina reflected. "Instead, it freed us. We're better friends now than we were for the last five years of pretending to be partners."

The Team Conversation

The conversation with Marta was different. Here, Katharina didn't need to end anything. She needed to offer something.

"I asked her to take a walk with me during lunch. And I just said, 'I've noticed you seem exhausted, and I've been avoiding saying anything because I don't know what to offer. But I'd rather have an awkward conversation than watch you burn out without trying to help'."

Marta cried. Not because the observation was painful, but because someone had finally seen her. She'd been afraid that admitting struggle would mark her as weak, uncertain whether Katharina would support her or judge her.

"What surprised me," Katharina said, "was how simple the solutions were once we named the problem. Marta didn't need a complete restructure. She needed permission. Permission to say no to projects that would push her over the edge. Permission to take a real vacation. Permission to be excellent without being superhuman."

Together, they redesigned Marta's role. Reduced client load. Added a junior creative director to share the burden. Created explicit permission for Marta to decline projects that would push her past sustainable capacity. None of this was expensive or complicated. It just required the conversation that neither of them had been willing to start.

The Family Conversation

The conversation with her mother was the hardest. Professional conversations have structures and boundaries. Family conversations carry decades of history and patterns.

Katharina invited her mother for a weekend. Not the usual rushed dinner between obligations, but an actual visit with time to breathe. On the second evening, over schnitzel at Figlmüller, despite being a bit of a tourist trap, a restaurant her father had loved, she finally answered the question she'd been deflecting for years.

"I told her I was lonely. That I wanted what she was asking about. That I didn't know why I hadn't made it happen, but I knew avoiding her questions wasn't helping either of us." Katharina's voice caught when she recounted this. "And she just took my hand across the table and said, 'I wasn't asking because

I disapproved of your life. I was asking because I worried you were unhappy, and I didn't know how to help. A mother just wants her daughter to be happy.'"

The conversation didn't solve Katharina's loneliness. But it transformed her relationship with her mother into something genuine. She'd traded the protection of deflection for the vulnerability of truth, and what she received in return was actual connection.

"The strangest thing," Katharina told me months later, "is that having those conversations didn't just fix the specific problems. It changed how I move through the world. I'm less afraid now, not of difficult topics, but of myself. I know I can face things I used to run from. That knowledge shows up everywhere, not just in the conversations I've already had, but in my willingness to have new ones."

What I Wish I'd Known: Avoidance Accumulates

If I could go back to my younger self, the one who believed that avoiding difficult conversations was a form of kindness or professionalism, I would offer this:

The conversations you avoid don't disappear. They accumulate. Every truth not spoken becomes a small wall between you and the people who matter to you. Over time, those walls become prisons that isolate you from the very connections you were trying to protect.

The discomfort of a difficult conversation is temporary. The discomfort of living with its absence is permanent. A complicated conversation might take an hour. Avoiding it shapes years.

People rarely leave relationships because of difficult conversations. They leave because of the accumulation of conversations that never happened. The truth, spoken with care, is almost always less damaging than the silence that replaces it.

I think of my own avoided conversations during the years before my breakdown. The times I didn't tell my team I was struggling. The times I performed certainty when I felt only confusion. The times I chose professional distance over vulnerable connection. Each silence seemed like protection in the moment. Together, they created the isolation that eventually became unsustainable.

Most importantly: The conversation you're avoiding is rarely as bad as you imagine. We catastrophize about worst-case scenarios that seldom materialize. What usually happens is something much simpler. Two people finally see each other clearly and decide together what to do about what they see.

Sammenhæng requires speaking the truths that matter. Not cruelly, not carelessly, but with the recognition that coherent lives are built on authentic connections, and genuine connections require honest words.

The Conversation Inventory

Take fifteen minutes to complete this inventory of avoided conversations. Be honest with yourself. No one else needs to see this.

- **Professional Conversations:** What conversation with a colleague, partner, or team member have you been avoiding? What is the gap you're not naming? What are you protecting by staying silent?
- **Personal Conversations:** What conversation with a family member or friend needs to happen? What truth are you not speaking? How long have you been avoiding it?
- **Internal Conversations:** What conversation do you need to have with yourself? What are you not admitting about your own situation, desires, or struggles?
- **The Priority Conversation:** Looking at your inventory, which conversation would have the most impact on your sense of sammenhæng if you had it? What's the first step you could take this week to initiate that conversation?

Questions for Reflection

Transformational Question: "What conversation are you avoiding that would set you free?"

This question isn't about blame or obligation. It's an invitation to recognize that the silences we maintain often imprison us more than any words could. Freedom isn't always about what we do. Sometimes it's about what we finally say. Consider: What would change in your life if you had that conversation? Not the worst-case scenario you've been using to justify avoidance, but the realistic outcome. What may be possible?

Personal Awareness: What patterns do you notice in the conversations you avoid? Are they clustered around certain relationships, certain topics, or specific fears? What does this pattern tell you about what you're protecting?

Systemic Thinking: How does your organization or family system make difficult conversations harder or easier? What unspoken rules govern what can and cannot be discussed? What would change if those rules were made explicit and questioned?

Action-Oriented: If you committed to having one avoided conversation this week, which would it be? What's the smallest first step you could take to begin? What support would you need?

Integration: How might having the conversations you're avoiding affect other areas of your life? What becomes possible when you stop spending energy on maintaining silences?

The Path Forward

I'm walking back through Neubau as the Vienna evening settles in. The creative agencies and design studios are emptying, their occupants spilling into wine bars and restaurants, the day's work giving way to the night's connection. Somewhere above me, the elevator in Katharina's building is probably groaning its way up or down, carrying someone toward a conversation that will matter.

Katharina sent me a message last week, six months after our first meeting. The agency restructuring is complete. Marta is thriving in her redesigned role. Her mother is visiting again next month, and this time they've planned activities together rather than around each other. "The loneliness isn't gone," she wrote. "But it's different now. It's not a secret I'm keeping. It's a reality I'm working with. And that makes it feel more like a situation to address than a fate to accept."

This is what sammenhæng feels like when it begins to return: not perfection, but coherence. Not having everything figured out, but being honest about what remains uncertain. Not avoiding all difficulty, but meeting difficulty with the truth rather than with silence.

The conversations that matter aren't always the ones we want to have. But they're the ones that connect who we are to how we live. They're the threads that hold our different selves together. They're the difference between performing a life and living one.

Having the conversations that matter reveals what people need from us. Not our performance of strength or certainty, but our willingness to be present with them in complexity and uncertainty. In Chapter 11, we'll explore what happens when we finally understand what our people need from us, and why that understanding requires letting go of what we thought leadership meant.

11 What Your People Need from You

Shifting from control to clarity, and discovering that enough is more than plenty.

The Brooklyn Bridge at 5:47 a.m. is a different country than the one tourists visit at midday. No crowds shuffling between the cable stays, no couples posing for engagement photos against the Manhattan skyline, no cyclists weaving impatiently through pedestrian traffic. Just me and a handful of runners, our footsteps on the wooden planks creating a rhythm that feels almost ceremonial in the pre-dawn quiet.

I'm in New York for two days, meeting with a client whose situation has become urgent enough to warrant the trip. But I woke early, jet-lagged and restless, and found myself drawn to this bridge the way you're drawn to places that hold pieces of your history.

I have lived in this city for thirteen years. From twenty-six to thirty-nine, the years when you figure out who you're going to be, or at least who you're going to try to be. I walked this bridge hundreds of times: commuting to meetings in Lower Manhattan, clearing my head after difficult days, bringing visiting friends to see the view that never gets old, no matter how many times you've seen it. The East River below, black and silver in the early light. The skyline ahead, those silhouettes that announce "New York" to the world.

The city shaped me in ways I'm still understanding. It taught me to move fast, think faster, and never show weakness. It taught me that achievement was the price of admission and that slowing down meant falling behind. It taught me that the answer to every problem was more: more effort, more hours, more intensity, more control.

Standing here now, watching the sun begin to pink the sky behind the Manhattan towers, I can see how much of that teaching I've had to unlearn. The bridge feels the same, the cables still humming with their own frequency when the wind picks up, but I am not the person who used to cross it. That person believed that enough was never enough. That person would not have been awake at this hour by choice, savoring stillness. That person would have been checking emails, planning the day's conquests, and turning even a morning walk into an opportunity for optimization.

The man I'm meeting today reminds me of who I used to be. That's partly why I took this case. And partly why it unsettles me.

Jonathan sends a car to pick me up, which tells you something about him before you've even met. The driver knows exactly where to find me at the end of the bridge, which tells you Jonathan is precise about details. And when I arrive at his office in Midtown, a glass-walled corner suite on the forty-third floor of a building that announces serious money, he's already waiting in the lobby rather than having an assistant escort me up, which tells you he's anxious about this meeting in a way he's trying not to show.

"Peter." His handshake is firm, his eye contact direct, his posture the kind of confident-aggressive stance that private equity teaches its partners. Jonathan is forty-eight, tall, with a full head of black hair, silver-templed in a way that reads as distinguished rather than aging, dressed in the understated expensive way that New York finance favors. Everything about him communicates control.

"Thank you for coming," he says as we ride the elevator to his floor. "I know you don't usually travel for initial meetings."

"Your situation sounded urgent."

"Urgent." He considers the word as the elevator doors open onto a floor of glass offices and purposeful activity. "I suppose that's accurate. Though I'm still not entirely sure what the situation is."

His corner office has the view you'd expect: Central Park stretching north, the city arrayed around it like an offering. But Jonathan doesn't gesture toward the window or offer the usual commentary about the real estate. He closes the door, sits down across from me at a small conference table rather than behind his desk, and exhales in a way that suggests he's been holding his breath for longer than he realized.

"Three months ago, my wife told me she wanted a divorce, and we are now separated. Two months ago, my best portfolio manager gave notice. Last month, the CEO at our largest holding company said he needed to talk about 'leadership alignment.' And last week, my twenty-three-year-old daughter told me I'm the reason she's been in therapy for two years dealing with 'the emotional absence of her father.'" He pauses. "I'm starting to sense a pattern, but I don't understand exactly what I'm looking at, much less what to do about it."

The Pattern of Giving What You Have Instead of What They Need

What Jonathan was experiencing is one of the most painful realizations a successful leader can face: the discovery that you've been giving people the wrong things, not out of negligence or malice, but out of a genuine belief that what you had to offer was what they needed.

Over the next two hours, Jonathan's story emerged in the way these stories usually do: not as a linear narrative but as a series of revelations, each one illuminating something he hadn't previously seen.

His wife, Rebecca, hadn't left because he worked too much, though he did. She left because when he was present, he wasn't present. "She said I treated our marriage like a portfolio company," Jonathan told me, his voice catching slightly. "Quarterly check-ins to make sure metrics were on track. Strategic interventions when something seemed off. But no actual . . . she used the word 'inhabiting.' She said I never inhabited our life together. I just managed it. I have no idea what that actually means."

His portfolio manager, David, hadn't left for more money, though the competing offer was generous. He left because after seven years of exceptional performance, he still felt like he was being supervised rather than trusted. "Every deal had to go through Jonathan's filter," David had told the

HR partner in his exit interview. "Every decision needed his approval. I was forty-one years old, managing a billion-dollar portfolio, and I still felt like an associate waiting for the partner to sign off."

His CEO's concern about "leadership alignment" was really a concern about Jonathan's involvement in operational details that should have been delegated years ago. "He sends me articles about supply chain optimization at midnight," the CEO had reportedly said. "He has opinions about our factory floor layout in Vietnam. He's a brilliant investor, but he doesn't seem to understand that his job is to set direction and provide resources, not to run the company from his corner office in Manhattan."

And his daughter's revelation was perhaps the most painful of all. "She said I was always solving problems she didn't have," Jonathan said quietly. "Giving advice she didn't ask for. Providing for her future when what she needed was my presence in her present. She said she felt like a project!"

The pattern was clear once you saw it. Jonathan was generous, dedicated, and genuinely well-intentioned. But he was giving everyone in his life what he had to offer: analysis, direction, solutions, control. What they needed was something entirely different: trust, presence, autonomy, space to be themselves rather than recipients of his expertise.

The Idea of Enough

In Danish, we have a word that captures something American achievement culture fundamentally misunderstands: *nok*. It translates simply as "enough," but it carries a meaning that goes far deeper than mere sufficiency.

Nok isn't about settling for less or lowering your standards. It's about recognizing that more isn't always better. That there's an optimal amount of almost everything: attention, advice, involvement, control. And that exceeding that optimum doesn't create more value. It creates diminishing returns, or worse, active harm.

A parent who provides enough guidance helps their child develop judgment. A parent who provides too much guidance prevents that development. A leader who offers enough direction creates clarity. A leader who offers too much direction creates dependency. A partner who gives enough attention nurtures a connection. A partner who gives too much attention, particularly of the wrong kind, can feel like surveillance, or neediness, rather than love.

Jonathan had never learned nok. His entire career, his entire identity, had been built on the premise that more was always better. More analysis led to better decisions. More involvement led to better outcomes. More control led to better results. This premise had made him extraordinarily successful in specific domains. It had also made him increasingly ineffective in the domains that mattered most.

"The hardest thing you're going to hear," I told him that morning in his office, "is that the problem isn't that you're not giving enough. The problem is that you're giving too much of the wrong things and not enough of the right ones."

He stared at me for a long moment. Outside the window, a helicopter crossed the sky above Central Park, its sound muffled by the thick glass. "What are the right things?"

"That's what we need to find out. But it starts with understanding what people need, rather than assuming they need what you're naturally inclined to give."

Jonathan's question—"What are the right things?"—is exactly what this chapter explores. The concept of *nok* tells us that more isn't always better, but it doesn't tell us what people actually need. For that, we need a different framework.

The Need Hierarchy 2.0

Most leaders are familiar with Maslow's hierarchy of needs, the pyramid that moves from basic physiological requirements through safety, belonging, and esteem to self-actualization. But Maslow was describing individual human development. What people need from their leaders is related but distinct.

Through my work with executives across industries and cultures, I've developed the Need Hierarchy 2.0, a framework for understanding what people need from those who lead them, whether in professional or personal contexts.

Level One: Safety

Before anything else, people need to feel safe. Not just physically safe, but psychologically safe. They need to know that mistakes won't be catastrophic, that honesty won't be punished, that their basic security isn't constantly at risk. Leaders who create genuine safety create the foundation for everything else. Leaders who undermine safety, whether through volatility, unpredictability, or punitive responses to failure, make higher-level needs impossible to address.

Jonathan thought he provided safety. His compensation was generous, his job security was clear, and his benefits were excellent. But his team experienced constant low-level threat: the midnight emails suggesting he was always watching, the detailed questions about decisions that should have been theirs to make, the sense that any deviation from his expectations could trigger intervention. Financial safety isn't psychological safety. And without psychological safety, people can't bring their best thinking to complex problems.

Level Two: Clarity

Once safety is established, people need clarity about what's expected of them, what success looks like, and how their work connects to a larger purpose. They need to understand the boundaries within which they're operating and the criteria by which their contributions will be evaluated.

Jonathan provided plenty of direction, but direction isn't clarity. He told people what to do without helping them understand why. He set expectations without explaining the reasoning behind them. He provided solutions when what people needed was frameworks for developing their own solutions. His team knew what Jonathan wanted in any given moment, but they didn't have the deeper understanding that would allow them to anticipate needs, exercise judgment, or contribute independently.

Level Three: Autonomy

With safety and clarity in place, people need room to exercise their own judgment, make their own decisions, and own their own outcomes. They need to feel trusted, not just instructed. This is where Jonathan struggled most visibly. His intelligence and experience made it easy for him to see the correct answer, or at least a proper answer, in almost any situation. And his instinct was to provide that answer immediately, cutting off the messy process by which his people might have found their own way to a solution.

The cost of this was invisible in the short term but devastating over time. His team stopped developing. They learned to wait for his input rather than build their own views. They became executors of his vision rather than contributors to a shared enterprise. And the best ones, like David, eventually left to find environments where their judgment would be valued rather than overridden.

Level Four: Growth

People need to feel that they're developing, learning, and becoming more capable over time. They need challenges that stretch them, feedback that helps them improve, and opportunities that expand what's possible for them. A leader's job isn't just to get the current work done but to develop people's capacity for future work.

Jonathan's controlling style prevented the failures that enable learning. By catching every mistake before it happened, by providing answers before questions were fully formed, by optimizing every process according to his own expertise, he denied his people the productive struggle through which real development occurs. They were protected from failure. They were also protected from growth.

Level Five: Meaning

At the highest level, people need to feel that their work matters, that they're contributing to something larger than themselves, that their efforts have purpose beyond personal advancement. Leaders who can articulate compelling meaning and connect daily work to a larger purpose create engagement that transcends compensation or status.

Jonathan had meaning in abundance for himself. He was building something, creating value, leaving a legacy. But he'd never successfully transferred that meaning to others. His team understood what they were doing, but not why it mattered. They knew the financial targets but not the human purpose behind them. They were well-paid participants in someone else's vision rather than co-creators of shared meaning.

The Gap Between Giving and Receiving

When I walked Jonathan through this framework, something shifted in his expression. For the first time since we'd sat down, he looked not just concerned but genuinely curious.

"I've been giving Level Two when they need Level Three," he said slowly. "Direction when they need autonomy. Answers when they need trust."

"That's part of it. But it's more than just the wrong level. It's also too much of even the right things. There's an optimal amount of safety that enables risk-taking. Too much safety creates complacency. There's an optimal amount of clarity that enables action. Too much clarity becomes micromanagement. Every level has a nok, an enough. And you've been exceeding that enough consistently, probably your whole career."

He was quiet for a long moment, looking out at the park below. A jogger was making their way along the reservoir, tiny from this height, following the same path thousands of others would follow today. There's something about New York that makes individual effort feel both heroic and insignificant at the same time.

"My daughter said something similar," Jonathan finally said. "She said I gave her everything except the one thing she needed: permission to figure things out for herself. She said my help felt like a cage. A gilded cage, but still a cage."

"What did you say?"

"I didn't say anything. I didn't have a good answer." He turned back to face me. "That was the most honest moment we've had in years. Both of us were just sitting there, not knowing what to do. And somehow that felt more connecting than all the advice I'd given her over the years."

This is the paradox that high achievers like Jonathan struggle to grasp: Sometimes giving less creates more. Sometimes the absence of your contribution is more valuable than its presence. Sometimes what people need most from you is not your knowledge, your solutions, or your control. It's your restraint.

This paradox becomes sharper in an age of artificial intelligence. AI is designed to give more. Ask it a question, and it provides comprehensive analysis. Request feedback, and it offers detailed assessment across multiple dimensions. Seek direction, and it generates options, frameworks, scenarios. AI has no concept of *nok*. It's optimized to be maximally helpful, which means maximally present, maximally contributive, maximally involved.

Leaders who use AI to augment their leadership often amplify precisely the pattern that was already causing problems. Jonathan, for instance, had started using AI to generate even more detailed feedback for his team, more comprehensive analyses of their decisions, more thorough assessments of their work. The technology made him more efficient at the thing he was already doing too much of.

"I thought AI would help me scale my involvement," he told me. "I could review more, provide input on more decisions, catch more potential mistakes. What I didn't realize was that scaling my involvement was the last thing my team needed."

This is what AI fundamentally cannot provide: restraint. Judgment about when contribution helps and when it hinders. The insight to know that sometimes the most valuable thing you can offer is nothing at all. The capacity to sit with someone in uncertainty without solving it for them.

AI can give your people information. It cannot give them trust. It can provide analysis. It cannot provide autonomy. It can generate feedback. It cannot create the psychological safety that comes from knowing your leader believes in your judgment. It can offer endless options. It cannot offer *nok*.

What makes human leadership valuable in an AI age isn't the ability to provide more than the machines can provide. The machines will always win that competition. What makes human leadership valuable is the ability to provide less, strategically. To know when your team needs direction and when they need space. To discern when your daughter needs advice and when she needs presence. To practice the restraint that no algorithm is designed to practice.

Jonathan's breakthrough wasn't learning to use AI more effectively. It was learning to use himself more sparingly. The technology could handle the transactional, analytical, and informational aspects of leadership. What remained for him, what only he could provide, was the wisdom to know when those things were needed and when they weren't. The judgment to give *nok*, not more.

What I Wish I'd Known: More Isn't Always Better

If I could go back to my younger self, the one who was so proud of his work ethic and so confident that more effort was always the answer, I would offer this:

The people around you don't need everything you have to give. They need what they need, which is often different from what you're naturally inclined to offer. Your job isn't to maximize your contribution. It's to calibrate your contribution to what serves them best.

Your worth isn't measured by how much you do. It's measured by what becomes possible because of how you lead. Sometimes what becomes possible requires you to do more. Often, particularly as you grow more senior and your people grow more capable, what becomes possible requires you to do less.

Nok isn't settling. It's the recognition that there's an optimal amount of almost everything and exceeding that optimum doesn't create more. It destroys while creating the illusion of dedication.

The greatest gift you can give the people you lead is trust: trust that they can figure things out, trust that they can recover from failures, trust that they can grow into challenges that stretch them. And trust requires restraint. You can't trust people while simultaneously controlling them.

I think about my years in New York, walking that bridge, building my career on the premise that more was always better. I was successful by every metric that mattered then. And I nearly destroyed myself proving how much I could give. Learning not to learn, knowing that enough is enough, wasn't a reduction of my ambition. It was an evolution of my being.

Cross-Cultural Assumptions About Leadership Giving

Different cultures have different assumptions about what leaders should provide, and understanding these variations can help leaders develop more flexible approaches to meeting people's actual needs.

- **The American Achievement Model.** American leadership culture often assumes that more is always better: more direction, more feedback, more involvement, more optimization. The ideal leader in this model is intensely engaged, always available, and constantly driving improvement. Jonathan was a perfect product of this culture. His intensity was rewarded throughout his career, reinforcing behaviors that were becoming increasingly counterproductive. The limitation of this model is that it treats leadership as an input problem, if more leadership input produces better outcomes. But leadership is an output problem: The goal is to create conditions for others to produce great work, and sometimes that requires less input rather than more.

- **The Scandinavian Trust Model.** Nordic leadership cultures tend to assume that people are capable until proven otherwise. The leader's job is to set direction and remove obstacles, then trust people to execute. Micromanagement is seen not as diligence but as a failure of trust. This model can feel uncomfortably hands-off to American leaders, but it often produces more sustainable results over time because it develops capability rather than dependence.
- **The German Precision Model.** German leadership culture often emphasizes clear systems and processes that reduce the need for constant managerial involvement. Once roles are defined and processes are established, people are expected to execute with minimal supervision. The leader's job is to design sound systems, not to be constantly present in their operation.
- **The Asian Relationship Model.** Many Asian business cultures emphasize relationships and mutual obligation over transactional management. Leaders are expected to know their people deeply, to invest in relationships that transcend specific work tasks, and to create loyalty through genuine personal connection rather than through constant oversight.

Jonathan had succeeded in a system that rewarded his style. But that system was changing, and even within his own organization, people from different cultural backgrounds experienced his intensity very differently. His Asian colleagues found his directness jarring. His European hires felt micromanaged. His younger American team members, raised with different expectations about autonomy and work-life boundaries, experienced his always-on style as invasive rather than dedicated.

The leaders who thrive across cultures are not those who impose their style uniformly, but those who read what different people need and adjust accordingly. Nok isn't a fixed quantity. It varies by person, by culture, by context, by relationship. The skill is in reading the situation accurately and calibrating your contribution to what's needed.

Leader Spotlight: The CEO Who Learned to Step Back

Mirjam ran a logistics company in Rotterdam, and when I met her, she was struggling with a familiar problem: Her best people kept leaving, and the ones who stayed seemed increasingly passive.

"I promoted my operations director last year," she told me. "Smart, capable, exactly the kind of leader we need. Within six months, he'd stopped making any decision without checking with me first. I don't understand it. I gave him the title, the authority, the compensation. Why won't he lead?"

We did an exercise together. For one week, Mirjam tracked every interaction she had with her direct reports: every email, every meeting, every informal conversation. Then we analyzed the pattern.

What emerged was striking. In almost every interaction, Mirjam was adding something: a suggestion, a refinement, an additional consideration, a question that was really a direction in disguise. Her additions were almost always valuable. Her instincts were almost always correct. And the cumulative effect was a team that had learned to wait for her input before acting.

"I think I understand," Mirjam said slowly. "By always adding something, I've trained them to need me to add something. They're not passive. They're adaptive. They've learned that the path of least resistance is to wait for my contribution."

We designed an experiment. For one month, Mirjam would practice "the discipline of restraint." When someone brought her a problem, she would ask questions rather than offer solutions. When someone proposed an approach, she would let it proceed even if she saw ways to improve it. When she felt the urge to add anything, she would pause and ask herself: "Is my contribution necessary, or am I making it because adding something is my habit?"

The first two weeks were excruciating. Mirjam watched decisions get made that weren't quite as good as the ones she would have made. She saw inefficiencies that she could have prevented. She experienced the discomfort of restraint when every instinct told her to engage.

But then something shifted. Her operations director started making faster decisions. Her team began solving problems at their level rather than escalating everything. And paradoxically, the quality of decisions improved because people were thinking rather than waiting to be told what to think.

"I had been addicted to being needed," Mirjam reflected afterward. "Every time I added to what we were doing, I got a little hit of importance. I was indispensable. But my indispensability was making everyone else dispensable, or dependent on me at least. I was the only one growing because I was the only one being challenged to think."

Three years later, Mirjam's company has grown 40%, with half the management overhead of comparable competitors. Her operations director now runs a major division with complete autonomy. And Mirjam spends most of her time on strategic development rather than operational involvement.

"The best thing I ever did for my company," she told me, "was learn to do less."

An Experiment in Giving Less

Jonathan and I spent two days in New York together, walking and talking through what a different approach might look like. By the time I left, Jonathan had committed to "the hardest thing I've ever tried": a deliberate practice of giving less, which might sound paradoxical, I know.

For his team, this meant: No more midnight emails. Questions instead of directives. Explicit conversations about what level of involvement people wanted from him. A stated policy that his job was to set direction and provide resources, not to optimize every decision.

For his daughter, this meant listening without solving and asking about her experience rather than providing his analysis of her situation and letting silences exist without filling them with advice and being present rather than productive.

For his marriage, it was too late. Rebecca had already moved on. But Jonathan began the process of understanding what had gone wrong, not to fix the relationship that was ending but to become capable of a different kind of relationship if the opportunity ever arose again.

Seven months later, he sent me a message. His daughter had asked him to go hiking, something they'd never done together. They'd spent three hours on a trail in the Hudson Valley, not talking about anything really, just walking and occasionally commenting on the trees or the weather or the other hikers they passed.

"It was the best conversation we've had in years," he wrote. "And we barely said anything. I'm starting to understand what she meant about my help feeling like a cage. I was so busy giving her what I had that I never asked what she needed. Turns out what she needed was space. Space to figure things out, space to fail, space to be herself without me constantly trying to improve her."

He added a postscript: "I think I finally understand what nok means. That you don't have to fill every silence, solve every problem, optimize every situation. Sometimes the best contribution is the one you don't make."

The Science Behind Calibrated Leadership

Research across psychology, economics, and organizational behavior reveals a consistent pattern: More isn't always better, and the most capable leaders often struggle most with calibration.

- **Self-Determination Theory.** Edward Deci and Richard Ryan's research at the University of Rochester established that intrinsic motivation requires three conditions: autonomy, competence, and relatedness. When leaders over-contribute, particularly through excessive direction, they undermine autonomy, which undermines motivation. Your people need enough guidance to feel competent, not so much that they feel controlled.
- **Psychological Safety and Voice.** Amy Edmondson's research at Harvard shows that teams with high psychological safety outperform those with low psychological safety, particularly on complex tasks that require innovation. But psychological safety isn't just about permission to speak. It's about leaders who create space for others to contribute, which often means they contribute less themselves.
- **Crowding Out Effects.** Economists have documented how external rewards can "crowd out" intrinsic motivation. The same principle applies to leadership involvement: When leaders are too present, they

can crowd out the independent thinking and initiative that produce the best outcomes.

- **The Dunning-Kruger Reversal.** Research shows that highly competent leaders are often the worst at calibrating their involvement. Their expertise makes them confident in their ability to add value, and that confidence can close their eyes to the costs of their constant contributions. The most capable people often have the hardest time recognizing when their capability becomes counterproductive.

The research points to something counterintuitive: Leadership effectiveness often increases as leaders learn to do less, not more. Calibration, not maximization, is the skill that matters.

The Need Audit

Take fifteen minutes to audit your giving patterns with the three people who depend on you most, whether at work or at home.

For each person, ask:

- What do I typically give them? (Be specific: direction, advice, solutions, time, attention, resources, control, etc.)
- What do they need from me? (Not what they need in general, but specifically from me in my role.)
- What might they need that I'm not giving? (Consider asking them directly.)
- Where might I be giving too much? (What contributions might be preventing their development or crowding out their initiative?)

The Restraint Experiment: Choose one relationship where you suspect you might be giving too much. For one week, practice deliberate restraint: Ask questions instead of offering answers, create space instead of filling it, trust instead of controlling. Notice what changes in the relationship and in your own experience.

Questions for Reflection

Transformational Question: "Are you leading for their growth or your comfort?"

This question cuts to the heart of why we over-give. Often, our excessive involvement isn't really about serving others. It's about managing our own anxiety, confirming our own worth, and maintaining our sense of being needed. When you ask whether you're leading for their growth or your comfort, you begin to see how much of your contribution is about you.

Personal Awareness: What needs are you meeting for yourself when you over-contribute? What anxiety are you managing by staying so involved? What would you have to confront about yourself if you stepped back?

Systemic Thinking: How does your organization reward or punish restraint? What signals does your culture send about the value of busyness versus effectiveness? What would change if leaders were evaluated on the growth of their people rather than their personal contribution?

Action-Oriented: Where could you practice restraint this week? What contribution could you withhold to see what emerges in its absence? What question could you ask instead of what answer could you give?

Integration: How do your patterns of over-giving at work show up in your personal relationships? Where else in your life might not create more be better?

Crossing the Bridge to the Other Side

I'm back on the Brooklyn Bridge, this time in the late afternoon, watching the sun begin its descent toward New Jersey. The bridge is crowded now: tourists, commuters, cyclists, runners, street vendors selling art and souvenirs. The solitude of dawn has given way to the chaos of a city in motion.

Jonathan walked with me to the bridge before I left for the airport. He wanted to see where I'd started my morning, to understand something about the place that had shaped me and was now part of his own story.

"I built my career on the opposite of nok," he said as we looked out at the water. "I believed that the answer to every problem was more. More effort, more control, more contribution. And now I'm learning that the answer might be less. Less interference. Less solving. Less me."

"The less you do," I said. "Not less you being. There's a difference. Nok isn't about withdrawing or becoming passive. It's about being fully present without needing to control. It's about trusting that your presence is valuable even when your production isn't required."

He nodded slowly, watching a ferry make its way toward Governors Island. "That's what my daughter was asking for, wasn't it? Not less of me. Less of what I was doing to her. She wanted me present. She just didn't want me productive."

This is the paradox that high achievers must navigate: We've built our identities on what we do, and learning that our doing might be the problem feels like an attack on who we are. But it's not. It's an invitation to discover that we're valuable for reasons beyond our output. That our presence matters independently of our production. That sometimes the greatest gift we can give is the space for others to discover what they're capable of without us.

Jonathan has a long way to go. Patterns built over decades don't dissolve in days. But he's started the journey from giving what he has to giving what's needed. From more to nok. From control to trust.

Understanding what people need from us is the foundation for something larger: designing a life we don't want to escape from. When we stop exhausting ourselves by over-giving, when we learn that enough is enough, we create space for something new. We make the possibility of a life that doesn't require recovery because it doesn't create depletion. That's where we're heading next.

12 A Life You Don't Want to Escape From

Designing your days around what matters, and discovering the joy that was waiting all along.

The scrape of metal stools on concrete. The thump of wooden crates being stacked at the vegetable stall. A vendor calling something to a colleague in rapid Danish, words bouncing off the ceiling of Torvehallerne. Somewhere nearby, the crinkle of waxed paper as someone wraps a wedge of aged cheese, and the tap-tap-tap of a card reader processing the first transactions of the day: morning sounds, unremarkable sounds, the acoustic texture of a city waking into its routines.

I'm watching the stream of children crossing Israel's Plads toward Zahles, an elementary and high school, backpacks bouncing, jackets zipped against the September chill. Some hold parents' hands. Others cluster in small groups, voices carrying across the square in fragments. I remember walking my own son to school years ago, a different school then, those mornings when his hand fit easily in mine and the route felt like our private ritual.

He goes to Zahles now, older, independent, spending most of his time with friends, the way teenagers should. On special occasions, I still get to do things with him, and those moments feel like gifts. But the daily walks, the small conversations about nothing important that were somehow important anyway, those belong to a different season now.

I find myself missing them more than I expected to. The ritual of it, repeated so many times it felt permanent, until suddenly it wasn't.

This is what they don't tell you about presence: You don't always know which moments matter until they're behind you. The ordinary days accumulate into a childhood, and then the childhood is over, and you're left hoping you were there for enough of it. Hoping that when your son thinks back on those years, he remembers a father who showed up. Not just physically, but fully. Present in the way that presence requires.

I'm early for my meeting, which gives me time to do what I've learned to do in the years since my breakdown: nothing much—just sitting with coffee, watching life unfold, letting thoughts arrive and depart without trying to capture them. The old me would have used these minutes to check emails, review notes, and optimize the waiting. The current me understands that sometimes the waiting is the point.

Maja arrives in the unmistakable state of someone who has just executed a successful school drop-off. Slightly rushed, slightly relieved, a small stain on her sweater that she either hasn't noticed or has decided not to care about. She carries a worn leather bag that I know contains at least three items her children forgot to pack this morning.

"All three delivered," she says, sliding into the chair across from me with the exhale of minor victory. "Oskar forgot his football boots, which means I'll be bringing them to school at lunch, but that's a problem for future Maja. Present Maja has earned a coffee."

She orders a cortado, and we sit for a moment watching another wave of children cross toward Zahles. One of them waves at the window, and Maja waves back.

"Freja's friend," she explains. "We did a playdate last week that somehow involved glitter in places glitter should never be. I'm still finding it in the sofa cushions." She says this without frustration, with something closer to wonder. "Three years ago, I would have been stressed about the boots, annoyed about the glitter, resentful about the interruption to my morning. Now it's just . . . life. The actual texture of the life I chose."

This is why I'm here. Not because Maja is in crisis, but because she isn't. After two years of working together, she's become something I don't have many examples of in my practice yet: a completion. Someone who has moved through fragmentation into genuine integration, who is now living proof that the journey this book describes leads somewhere worth going.

The Before and After

When Maja first came to me, she was running a successful restaurant in Vesterbro and systematically destroying her health, her marriage, and her relationship with her children in the process. She didn't see it that way, of course. She saw herself as building something meaningful, making sacrifices that would eventually pay off, doing what successful founders do.

Her restaurant had become a critic's darling within eighteen months of opening. The reviewers loved her commitment to local sourcing, her inventive combinations, and her refusal to choose between sustainability and flavor. What they didn't see was Maja leaving for the restaurant before her children woke and returning after they slept. What they didn't see was her husband, Tomás, increasingly managing the household alone while she pursued excellence. What they didn't see was a woman who had built something beautiful by hollowing herself out.

"I remember the moment I realized something had to change," she tells me now, her cortado cooling between her hands. "Freja, my oldest, she was five at the time, asked Tomás if Mommy still lived with them. Not in a sad way. In a genuinely curious way, like she wasn't sure. That's when I understood that I wasn't sacrificing for my family. I was sacrificing my family."

The work we did together wasn't about reducing her ambition. Maja's drive was part of who she was and squashing it would have created a different kind of fragmentation. Instead, we worked on integration: how to bring her whole self to both her work and her family, how to build systems that didn't require her constant presence, how to redefine success in terms that included sustainability.

Two years later, the results speak for themselves. The restaurant is still thriving, now with a head chef who runs the kitchen four nights a week while Maja focuses on development. She's built a test kitchen in a converted space near Israels Plads, where she develops new concepts with a small team. And in three months, she's opening her second restaurant in Madrid, with a London location planned for next year.

"The expansion would have been impossible before," she says. "Not because of the business complexity, but because I would have tried to do everything myself. I would have been in Madrid every week, obsessing over every detail, missing my children's lives while telling myself it was temporary. Now I have systems. I have people I trust. I have boundaries that are actual boundaries, not suggestions I ignore when things get intense."

She pauses, watching a barista craft something elaborate for a customer who seems to be photographing every step of the process.

"But the real change isn't the business structure. It's me. I used to think life was something that happened in the gaps between work. Now I understand that work is something that happens within life. The order matters."

The Joy That Was Waiting

In Danish, we have a word that captures what Maja has found: *livsglæde*. It translates literally as "life joy," but its meaning runs deeper than simple happiness. Livsglæde is the fundamental appreciation for life itself, independent of achievement or status or external validation. It's the joy that comes from being alive, not from what you've accomplished with your life.

For high achievers like Maja, and like me, and perhaps like you, livsglæde is surprisingly difficult to access. We've spent so long deriving our sense of worth from what we produce that we've forgotten how to be simple. We know how to chase joy through accomplishment. We're less practiced at receiving joy through presence.

The irony is that livsglæde was always available. It wasn't something we needed to earn or achieve. It was waiting for us to stop moving long enough to notice it. The joy of a September morning. The weight of a child's backpack on your shoulder. The smell of coffee and bread and possibility. The unremarkable moments that, accumulated, constitute an actual life.

I've thought a lot about why this is so difficult for people like us. Part of it is training. We've been taught that happiness is earned, that rest must be deserved, that enjoying life without constantly improving it is somehow lazy or complacent. Part of it is identity. When your sense of self is built on what you produce, stopping production feels like stopping existence. And part of it is fear. Fear that if you slow down, everything will fall apart. Fear that the success you've built requires constant vigilance to maintain.

"I used to think I'd be happy when the restaurant was successful," Maja says. "Then, when it was successful, I thought I'd be happy when it was stable. Then, when it was stable, I thought I'd be happy when I could expand. There was always a next threshold, and happiness was always on the other side of it."

She looks out at the square, where the last stragglers are making their way toward school.

"What I've learned is that the threshold was imaginary. The happiness was here all along. I just wasn't available to receive it. I was so focused on building a life I could eventually enjoy that I wasn't living the life I already had."

This is what integration makes possible: not a smaller life with less ambition, but a fuller life with more presence. Maja hasn't reduced her goals. She's pursuing a larger vision than she was two years ago. But she's seeking it from a different place, not from scarcity and fear, but from abundance and joy, and not sacrificing the present for a future that keeps receding, but building a future that includes the present she wants to live.

The Science Behind Sustainable Success

The approach this book advocates isn't just philosophically appealing. It's supported by substantial research on human flourishing.

- **The Harvard Study of Adult Development.** Running for over eighty years, this is one of the longest studies of adult life ever conducted. Its primary finding is unambiguous: The quality of our relationships is the strongest predictor of health and happiness across the lifespan. Not achievement, not wealth, not status. Relationships.
- **The U-Curve of Happiness.** Research across cultures shows that happiness tends to follow a U-shaped curve across the lifespan,

bottoming out in the mid-forties before rising again. One explanation is that midlife is when people begin releasing unrealistic expectations and accepting life as it is. Those who resist this acceptance, continuing to chase external validation indefinitely, often remain stuck at the bottom of the curve.

- **The Three Human Needs.** Decades of research show that sustainable well-being comes from satisfying three basic needs: autonomy (the feeling of choice and self-direction), competence (the experience of effectiveness and mastery), and relatedness (connection with others). Achievement culture tends to overemphasize competence while undermining autonomy and relatedness.
- **The Paradox of Ambition.** Studies on goal achievement show that people who achieve their primary life goals often experience a phenomenon called "arrival fallacy," the disappointment that follows achieving something you expected to make you happy. The research suggests that well-being comes more from the process of pursuing meaningful goals than from reaching them.
- **Recovery and Performance.** Sports science research demonstrates that recovery is not separate from performance but essential to it. Athletes who train continuously without adequate recovery perform worse than those who integrate rest into their regimens. The same principle applies to cognitive and emotional work: Sustainable high performance requires sustainable recovery.

The Life Design Canvas

When I work with leaders who are ready to move from fragmentation to integration, I use a framework called the Life Design Canvas. It's not a productivity tool or a goal-setting exercise. It's a way of making visible the life you're designing, whether intentionally or by default.

The canvas has five domains, each representing an essential dimension of a whole human life.

Domain One: Vitality

This is the foundation. Your physical energy, health, sleep, movement, and nutrition. Without vitality, everything else becomes a struggle. With it, challenges become manageable. Most high achievers sacrifice this domain first, treating their bodies as machines to be optimized rather than living systems to be nourished.

Maja's vitality had been devastated by her restaurant schedule. She was sleeping five hours a night, eating standing up between services, and relying on adrenaline to compensate for genuine rest. Rebuilding vitality became the foundation of everything else. Better sleep creates better thinking. Better thinking created better decisions. Better decisions created space for everything that followed.

Domain Two: Connection

The relationships that sustain us. Partner, family, close friends, community. These are not optional additions to a successful life. They are the infrastructure that makes everything else meaningful. Achievement without connection is a hollow victory. Connection without achievement can still be a rich life.

For Maja, connection had become the casualty of her ambition. She was technically married but functionally alone. She had children she barely knew. She had colleagues but few actual friends. Rebuilding connection meant being present, not just physically but emotionally. It meant having conversations that weren't about work. It meant being home for bedtime, not as an occasional treat but as an actual practice.

Domain Three: Contribution

The work that matters to you. Not just employment, but the expression of your capabilities in service of something beyond yourself. For Maja, this was her restaurant, her food, her creative vision. For others, it might be leading a team, building a company, teaching, creating art, or raising children. Contribution is how we express our gifts in the world.

The goal isn't to reduce contribution but to right-size it. To give enough without depleting yourself. To contribute in ways that generate energy rather than consume it. Maja discovered that she could contribute more by doing less, because the less she did was the work only she could do, while the more she delegated went to people who often did it better than she would have.

Domain Four: Growth

The ongoing development of yourself as a human being. Learning, challenging, becoming more than you were. High achievers often confuse professional development with personal growth, but they're not the same thing. You can advance your career while stagnating as a person. You can maintain the same job title while growing profoundly in knowledge, self-understanding, and capability.

Maja's growth had been entirely focused on her craft. She was becoming a better chef while becoming a less developed human. Our work together expanded her definition of growth to include emotional intelligence, relational capability, self-awareness, and the kind of wisdom that comes from reflecting on experience rather than just accumulating it.

Domain Five: Presence

The capacity to be here, in this moment, living the life that's happening rather than the life you're planning or remembering. Presence is what makes all the other domains available to you. Without it, you can have vitality but not feel alive, have connections but not feel connected, make contributions but not feel fulfilled.

This was Maja's greatest struggle and her most significant transformation. Learning to be present didn't mean becoming passive or abandoning her drive. It meant experiencing her life as it happened rather than constantly planning the next phase or worrying about what might go wrong. It meant tasting her own food instead of just evaluating it and seeing her children instead of just managing them and being in her marriage instead of just maintaining it.

What I Wish I'd Known: It's Already Here

If I could go back to my younger self, the one who believed that life was something you built and happiness was something you earned, I would offer this:

The life you're trying to build is already here. It's happening while you're busy planning the next phase. It's in the morning light through a window, in the weight of your child's hand, in the taste of coffee that you drink too fast to experience. The question isn't how to create a life worth living. It's how to be present for the life you already have.

Achievement is not the enemy. Ambition is not the problem. The problem is when achievement becomes a substitute for living rather than an expression of it. The problem is when ambition crowds out presence rather than being integrated with it. You don't have to choose between success and fulfillment. But you do have to design for both intentionally, because the default is a life that optimizes for achievement while neglecting everything else.

Livsglæde isn't something you find after you've achieved enough. It's available in every moment, waiting for you to slow down enough to notice. The joy of being alive isn't a destination you reach. It's a capacity you develop. And like any capacity, it grows with practice and atrophies with neglect.

I think about my own breakdown, five years ago now. At the time, it felt like the end of everything I'd worked for. I'd lost my company, my identity, my sense of who I was and what I was capable of. The months that followed were the darkest of my life. But they were also the beginning of everything that has come since. The collapse was not a failure. It was an invitation to build something different. Something more integrated, more sustainable, more alive.

The life you don't want to escape from isn't built by escaping your current life. It's built by inhabiting your current life more fully, by being present for what's already here while working toward what you want to create. The integrated life isn't a future state you'll achieve when conditions are right. It's a present practice you begin when you decide that waiting is no longer acceptable.

What I wish I'd known is that the life I was running toward was never going to satisfy me, because satisfaction doesn't come from arrival. It comes from presence. From being here, in this moment, with these people, doing this work. The life I don't want to escape from isn't a life without problems or stress or challenges. It's a life where I'm fully present for all of it. The difficulties and the joys. The achievements and the struggles. The ordinary moments that, accumulated, constitute the only life I'll ever have.

What Integration Actually Looks Like

After finishing our coffees, Maja and I walk across Israels Plads toward her test kitchen. The morning has warmed slightly, and the square is filling with the usual Copenhagen mix: parents with strollers, professionals on bicycles, tourists studying maps with the focused intensity of people trying to find hygge.

The test kitchen occupies a converted retail space, an old pharmacy, with wooden built-in cabinets and high ceilings, the kind of building that Copenhagen has many of and knows how to repurpose beautifully. A small team is already at work when we arrive, prepping ingredients for a new menu concept that will eventually travel to Madrid.

"Three years ago, I would have been here at five-thirty," Maja says as we walk through. "I would have been prepping alongside them, checking every cut, tasting every element. I told myself it was quality control. Really, it was an inability to trust. Inability to let go."

She stops to greet her team, asking questions about their process, making a suggestion about one technique that is genuinely collaborative rather than controlling. They respond to her with the easy familiarity of people who feel trusted rather than supervised.

"Now I come in at eight-thirty, after the kids are at school. I leave at four, before pickup. I'm here for the important decisions, the creative direction, and the problem-solving that requires me. Everything else, they handle. And they handle it well because I let them learn, even when that meant letting them make mistakes I could have prevented."

We settle in a small office at the back of the kitchen, where a window overlooks the prep area. I can see her watching her team with an expression I've come to recognize: the quiet peace of a leader who has learned to trust.

"The Madrid opening," I ask. "How are you managing that without falling back into old patterns?"

She laughs, a nervous laugh that acknowledges the difficulty of the question. "It's a daily practice. The urge to control everything is still there. The voice that says I should be doing more, that I'm not working hard enough, that success requires sacrifice. That voice doesn't go away. I've just learned not to obey it automatically."

She explains the structure she's built: a capable partner in Madrid who has full operational authority, weekly video calls for strategic alignment, monthly visits that are intensive but bounded, clear metrics for success that don't require her constant presence to monitor.

"The old me would be there every week. The old me would be reviewing every vendor contract, tasting every dish, attending every staff meeting. And the old me would miss Oskar's football matches and Freja's school play and the thousand small moments that constitute my children's childhoods." She pauses. "I'm not willing to miss those anymore. And I've learned that I don't have to. The choice between success and presence was always false. I just believed it because everyone around me seemed to believe it."

I ask about Tomás, her husband, and how the relationship has weathered her transformation. She smiles. Tomás is from Barcelona originally, and their family splits holidays between Copenhagen and Catalonia, their children growing up fluent in Danish and Spanish. It's part of why Madrid makes sense for the expansion: Tomás has connections there, understands the market, and the family already has roots in that direction.

"We almost didn't make it. The first year was hard. He'd spent so long managing everything at home that he didn't quite trust my change was real. He kept waiting for me to revert, for the restaurant to consume me again. And honestly, I kept worrying the same thing."

She picks up a pencil from her desk, turns it over in her hands, the kind of fidgeting that happens when someone is being more honest than comfortable.

"What saved us was talking about it and saying the things we'd avoided saying for years. I had to acknowledge how much I'd hurt him, how much

I'd been absent, how unfair it was that I'd expected him to carry everything at home while I chased my dream. He had to acknowledge his own resentments, his own compromises, the ways he'd enabled my patterns by not confronting them sooner. It wasn't easy. But it was necessary."

Now, she says, they're more partners than they've been since before the restaurant opened. They share household responsibilities in ways they never did when she was working hundred-hour weeks. They have date nights that happen, conversations that aren't about logistics, a connection that exists independently of the children who occupy so much of their daily attention.

"The marriage is better than it was before we opened, not despite the restaurant, but because of everything I had to learn to keep both. The crisis forced growth that never would have happened otherwise. I wouldn't choose to go through it again. But I wouldn't undo it either."

Leader Spotlight: Three Paths to Integration

Maja's story is one version of what integration can look like. But the path to a life you don't want to escape from takes different forms for different people.

Henrik, the CEO we met in Chapter 1, eventually restructured not just his schedule but his entire company. He moved from a model where everything depended on his presence to one where his team could operate autonomously for weeks at a time. This allowed him to spend two months each year at his family's summer house in Sweden, working remotely but not constantly, present for his children in a way he'd never been during his years of building the business.

"I thought I was indispensable," he told me recently. "Turns out I was just unwilling to build a company that didn't need me. Once I got over my ego, everything became possible."

Elena, from Chapter 7, took a different path. After her recovery from burnout, she realized that her pharmaceutical career, successful as it was, had never been what she wanted. She'd pursued it to please her parents, to prove her capabilities, to achieve the kind of success that looks impressive on paper. At fifty-two, she left to start a small consultancy focused on helping other leaders avoid the burnout she'd experienced. We are "compcolleagues" now (competitors and colleagues at the same time). She makes a fraction of what she used to earn and describes herself as happier than she's ever been.

"The question isn't whether you're successful," she says now. "It's whether you're successful at something that matters to you. I was winning a game I didn't want to play. Now I'm playing my own game, and even on the hard days, it feels like mine."

And Jonathan, from Chapter 11, is still in the middle of his journey. His marriage ended, but his relationship with his daughter is slowly rebuilding. He's restructured his involvement at his firm, stepping back from the constant oversight that had characterized his leadership, creating space for others to grow. At the same time, he focuses on the strategic work that genuinely requires his capabilities.

"I'm not where I want to be," he told me last month. "But I'm moving in the right direction. And for the first time in my life, I'm present for the journey rather than just focused on the destination. I know it sounds corny, but it's true."

Technology Can't Help People Live

This is worth saying directly as we approach the end of this book: Artificial intelligence is, by design, an optimization tool. It can help you achieve more, produce more, accomplish more. It can make you more efficient at the things you're already doing. But it cannot help you live.

The things that constitute *livsglæde*, the joy of being alive, are not optimizable. The weight of your child's hand in yours. The taste of coffee when you're present to drink it. The conversation with a friend where neither of you is trying to accomplish anything. The morning light through a window that you notice because you're not already planning the next thing. These moments cannot be automated, delegated, or enhanced by technology. They can only be experienced by a human being who is present enough to receive them.

I've watched leaders use AI to become extraordinarily productive while becoming progressively less alive. They optimize their calendars, automate their communications, streamline their decisions. They accomplish more in a day than they used to accomplish in a week. And at the end of that day, they feel emptier than before. Because the life they're building with all that efficiency isn't a life they want to inhabit. It's a machine for producing outputs, not a home for a human being.

The question AI forces us to ask is not "How can I accomplish more?" We can all accomplish more now. The question is "What is worth accomplishing, and who do I want to be while accomplishing it?" AI handles the transactional. It manages the informational. It processes the analytical. What remains for humans is everything that makes a life worth living: presence, connection, meaning, joy.

This is the final paradox of the book. We live in an age where technology can handle more of the work than ever before. And that means the distinctly human work, the work of being present, of building relationships, of finding meaning, of experiencing *livsglæde*, becomes more important, not less. AI gives us the capacity to accomplish more with less effort. What we do with that recovered capacity determines whether we become more productive or more alive.

Maja chose to become more alive. She uses technology to run two restaurants across two countries while being home for her children's bedtimes. The efficiency serves the presence, not the other way around. The tools amplify her effectiveness so she can invest more deeply in what matters: her family, her craft, her health, her joy.

The Life Design Canvas

Take twenty minutes to assess your current life across the five domains. For each, rate your current state from 1 to 10 and identify one change that would increase your rating.

- **Vitality:** How is your physical energy? Sleep, nutrition, movement, rest? What one change would most increase your vitality?
- **Connection:** How are your key relationships? Partner, family, close friends, community? Where is the most significant gap between what you want and what you have?
- **Contribution:** Is your work aligned with your values and capabilities? Are you giving what only you can provide? What would make your contribution more sustainable?
- **Growth:** Are you developing as a person, not just as a professional? What kind of growth have you been neglecting?

- **Presence:** Are you living your life or just planning and reviewing it? What practices help you be more present?
- **The Integration Question:** Looking at your scores, where is the most significant imbalance? What would change if you addressed that imbalance, even partially, over the next three months?

Questions for Reflection

Transformational Question: "What would you create if you knew you couldn't fail?"

This question isn't about removing risk from your decisions. It's about revealing what you want when fear isn't making choices for you. What would your life look like if you designed it around genuine desire rather than anxiety about what might go wrong? What becomes possible when you stop preparing for failure and start creating for meaning?

Personal Awareness: When you imagine a life you don't want to escape from, what does it include? What's present that isn't present now? What's absent that currently dominates your time?

Systemic Thinking: What systems have you built, or allowed to develop, that keep you trapped in patterns you want to change? What would need to shift at a structural level for integration to become sustainable?

Action-Oriented: What one change could you make this week that would move you toward greater integration? What's the smallest step that would begin to shift your trajectory?

Integration: How would the people who depend on you be affected if you became more integrated? What would become possible for them if you were more present, more vital, more alive?

There Is No Escape, and That's as It Should Be

I leave Maja's test kitchen in the late morning, walking back through Israels Plads toward my own next meeting. The children who streamed toward Zahles hours ago are now inside classrooms, learning whatever children learn at that age. The square has filled with the mid-morning crowd: people on laptops at outdoor tables, a yoga class happening on the basketball court, someone practicing saxophone with more enthusiasm than skill.

Copenhagen does life well. It's not perfect, no city is, but there's a quality of presence here that I've found in a few other places. People seem less hurried, not because they're less ambitious, but because they've made different choices about what ambition means. Livsglæde isn't just a Danish concept. It's a Danish practice, visible in the way people move through their days, the priority they place on time with family and friends, and the collective agreement that success without quality of life isn't success.

I think about Maja watching her children cross this square toward school, about the life she's built that includes both a growing business empire and glitter in the sofa cushions. About the integration she's achieved that seemed impossible when she first sat in my office, exhausted and empty and certain that something had to change but unclear what.

She's not finished. None of us ever is. Integration isn't a destination you reach but a practice you maintain. There will be days when old patterns reassert themselves, when the voice that says "more" drowns out the concept of *nok*, when work crowds out presence, and achievement feels more urgent than connection. The difference is that now she sees those moments for what they are: temporary regressions, not permanent failures, invitations to return to the center rather than evidence that the center was always an illusion.

This is what I want for everyone who reads this book. Not perfection, but practice. Not a life without struggle, but a life where struggle serves growth. Not the absence of ambition, but ambition integrated with presence, achievement integrated with connection, success integrated with the fundamental joy of being alive.

The life you don't want to escape from isn't waiting for you in some imagined future. It's available now, in this moment, if you're willing to design for it. Suppose you're willing to make different choices than the ones that brought you here. If you're eager to believe that enough is enough, that presence is possible, that livsglæde isn't earned but received.

It begins, as all journeys do, with a single step. With the decision that something needs to change, and the recognition that you are the only one who can change it. With the courage to imagine a life worth inhabiting and the persistence to build it, one choice at a time, one day at a time, one moment of presence at a time.

This is not the end. It's an invitation. The work continues, the practice deepens, the integration evolves. In the conclusion that follows, I'll share some final reflections on my own ongoing journey and extend an invitation for yours.

Conclusion

An invitation to begin again.

The water is four degrees. I know this because I checked the temperature on the digital thermometer sitting on the dock, the way I do every morning, though it rarely changes my decision. I lower myself down the ladder, the cold gripping my ankles first, then my calves, then everything. The gasp comes automatically. It always does. For a few seconds, there is nothing in the world except this: the shock, the cold, the body's ancient alarm bells ringing. Then I push off and swim.

Twenty strokes out, twenty strokes back. That's all. Some mornings I stay longer, but today the cold is sharp, and I'm ready to climb out after a few minutes. I stand on the dock, water streaming off me, breath visible in the early air, and I feel what I always think after these swims: awake. Not the caffeinated alertness I used to mistake for energy, but something quieter. Present. Here.

I moved to this apartment not long ago. Through the window, the harbor stretches out in the early morning gray, a few boats making their way toward open water. Upstairs, my partner and my son are still sleeping. The day hasn't started demanding things from any of us yet. These early hours have become precious, a buffer between rest and responsibility where I can simply exist without producing. I didn't always value time like this. I used to see it as wasted. Now I see it as essential.

Before 2020, I couldn't have written this book. Not because I lacked the words, but because I hadn't yet lived the life. I was still the person who believed that success required sacrifice, that rest was earned through exhaustion, that slowing down meant falling behind. I was still running toward a future that kept receding, still measuring my worth by what I produced, still convinced that enough was never enough.

Then came the breakdown. And then came the long, slow work of rebuilding.

The Place Where I Learned to Stand Still

After the collapse, I retreated to a country house in the Danish countryside. Weeks stretched into months. I had no plan, no agenda, no idea what I was supposed to be doing. For the first time in my adult life, there was nothing on my calendar and no one expecting me to produce anything.

I walked. That's mostly what I did. Long walks through fields and forests, along paths that led nowhere, through weather that changed without warning. Some days, I walked for hours without seeing another person. Some days, I barely left the house at all. I learned to be alone with myself in a way I had spent decades avoiding.

There was a moment, standing at the edge of a field with the wind cutting across from the coast, when I realized I couldn't remember the last time my mind had been quiet and not distracted, not entertained, not focused on the next thing. Just quiet. The recognition frightened me. And then it freed me.

In that silence, I started to hear things I'd been drowning out with activity. The grief of a marriage that had ended. The exhaustion my body had been carrying. The emptiness that all my achievements had never touched. I had built a life that looked impressive from the outside and felt hollow from the inside. I had achieved everything I thought I wanted, only to find it wasn't what I wanted at all.

The walks didn't fix anything, not directly. But they created space for something to shift. They taught me that I could exist without producing, that my worth wasn't contingent on my output, that standing still wasn't the same as falling behind. They taught me to be present in a way that all my years of achievement had never required.

When I finally left that country house, I was not healed. I was not transformed into some serene version of myself who had transcended ambition. But I was different. Something had cracked open that couldn't be closed again. I had glimpsed another way of being, and I couldn't pretend I hadn't seen it.

The Small Revolutions

People sometimes ask me what's different now, and I find the question hard to answer. The changes are so woven into daily life that they've become invisible to me. But when I stop to think about it, I realize how much has shifted.

I don't get upset about standing in lines anymore. This sounds trivial, but it's not. For years, every queue was an affront, every delay a theft of time I could be using productively. I would check emails, make calls, draft messages, anything to avoid the unacceptable waste of simply waiting. Now I just wait. I notice things, the people around me, the sounds of the space, my own breathing. The line moves, or it doesn't. Either way, I'm not somewhere else in my head, wishing I was somewhere else in my body.

I work fewer hours and accomplish more of what matters. This isn't a productivity hack. It's the natural result of being clear about what matters and ruthless about what doesn't. I say no more often. I protect time for thinking and recovery. I've stopped confusing activity with progress.

I have honest conversations about not having answers. This was terrifying at first. My identity had been built on being the person who knew what to do. Admitting uncertainty felt like professional suicide. Instead, it turned out to be professional liberation. The leaders I work with don't need me to have all the answers. They need me to help them find their own.

I eat lunch. Sitting down and tasting the food. This sounds absurd even to mention, but for years, I ate standing up, or at my desk, or not at all. Food was fuel, and refueling was an interruption. Now I sit down. I taste things. Sometimes I even enjoy it.

I notice beauty more often. The light on the harbor in the morning. The sound of rain on the window. The soft green of Danish trees in early summer. I don't know whether the world became more beautiful or I became more attuned to seeing it. Either way, there's more wonder in ordinary days than I ever experienced when I was too busy achieving to pay attention.

What Can Change in a Few Weeks

I've watched people shift in a matter of days once they decide something has to give. A CEO who hasn't slept through the night in months starts sleeping again within two weeks of changing her evening routine. A founder who couldn't remember his last real conversation with his daughter rebuilds their connection in a single weekend of intentional presence. A managing director who's been white-knuckling through anxiety discovers that the thing he's been avoiding isn't as terrifying as the avoidance itself.

The initial shifts can happen fast. Sometimes remarkably fast. The body wants to heal. The mind wants clarity. The relationships wish to be repaired. When we stop actively working against ourselves, recovery can begin.

But the deeper work, the real integration, takes years. And it's probably never finished. The patterns we're unwinding were built over decades. They're woven into our identities, our relationships, our organizations, our cultures. You don't undo all of that in a weekend workshop or a three-month coaching engagement. You undo it slowly, imperfectly, over the course of a lifetime.

I'm still in that process. I still catch myself falling into old patterns. I still sometimes say yes when I mean no, still sometimes prioritize the urgent over the important, still sometimes forget that I'm a human being having an experience rather than a productivity machine that happens to have feelings. The difference is that I notice sooner. I correct faster. I forgive myself more readily. The practice isn't perfection. The practice is practice.

Still Becoming

I'm not writing this from some summit of integration where I've figured it all out. I'm writing it from the middle of my own ongoing work, still becoming, still learning, still sometimes getting it wrong.

The leaders I work with don't need gurus. They need companions. People who've walked some of the same path and can offer guidance without pretending to have transcended the struggle. That's what I can offer. Six companies across three countries. Two decades of building, failing, rebuilding. A breakdown that stripped away everything I thought defined me and the slow work of discovering what remained. Now I sit with founders and CEOs across more than a dozen countries, more than a hundred leaders who are navigating their own versions of the journey I've been on. Not perfection, but practice. Not answers, but better questions. Not a destination, but a direction.

Some readers will finish this book and wonder if what I'm describing is even possible. Can leaders really sustain effectiveness while maintaining their humanity? Can organizations really succeed without burning out their people? Can achievement and well-being coexist?

I believe they can. I've lived it, imperfectly, and I've watched leader after leader live it too. Not without struggle, not without setbacks, but genuinely. It's possible to lead without losing yourself. It's possible to achieve without sacrificing the life you're trying to build. It's likely to be whole.

The Invitation to Begin Again

This is my invitation to you: Begin again. Take one step. Ask one question. Have one conversation. Notice one thing you've been avoiding. Trust that the small steps accumulate, that the daily practices add up to a different life, that the person you want to become is not so far from the person you already are.

The harbor outside my window is brightening now. It's time for my day to begin, time to climb back up to the apartment where my partner and son are probably stirring, time to step into the ordinary rhythm of a life I've worked hard to build and no longer want to escape from.

When you close this book, I hope that you find your own version of the morning swim. Your own daily practice of presence. Your own small revolution against the fragmentation that achievement culture demands.

The whole human leader is not a destination. It's a direction. And you're already on your way.

Acknowledgments

Some books emerge fully formed. This one assembled itself slowly, across three countries and two decades of getting it wrong before getting it right.

To the team at Wiley, who reached out with an offer I genuinely thought was a phishing email. Thank you for being patient while I verified you were real, and for your guidance in shaping this book from initial concept to final manuscript.

To the leaders I've worked with across four continents—you trusted me with your breaking points and your breakthroughs. Every framework in this book emerged from our work together. You taught me as much as I taught you.

To the people who built companies with me over the years. We shaped another way of working together, even when I was still figuring out what that meant. From first hire to last, each of you contributed something essential to what became the Whole Human Approach—you just didn't know it at the time, and neither did I.

To those who picked up the phone in 2020 when I finally admitted I wasn't okay. You know who you are. You saved my life by simply listening without trying to fix me.

To my parents, who each taught me resilience and permitted me to find my own.

To Joanna, who anchors this whole human when he needs it.

To Theo, who reminds me daily that being present matters more than being productive.

About the Author

Peter Sorgenfrei is a Danish entrepreneur and leadership coach who has spent the last twenty-five years learning what sustainable success requires.

Born and raised in Copenhagen, Peter spent a year in Paris before university, working at Sony Music and auditioning to be Goofy at Disneyland Paris, and be part of a production for the American Ballet in Paris. (He didn't get either part.) He returned to complete his master's degree in economics from the University of Copenhagen.

In 2000, Peter moved to New York, working in strategic roles at DaimlerChrysler, Toyota, and as an equity analyst at UBS on Wall Street. In 2005, he left Wall Street to build his first company. Over the next fifteen years, he led six startups across Europe and North America.

In addition to New York and Paris, he has lived in London and Vienna, assembling teams across multiple countries and cultures, and learning both the exhilaration and the cost of relentless growth.

In 2020, his body forced him to stop. The breakdown that followed became the foundation for the Whole Human Approach now used by executives across four continents. He brings a Scandinavian perspective to leadership that questions the prevailing achievement culture's assumption that more is always better.

Peter coaches founders and CEOs globally, helping them build organizations that don't require people to fragment themselves to succeed. When he's not working, he's embarrassing his family with dad jokes and getting up before dawn to swim in the cold harbor of Copenhagen.

Work still consumes him sometimes. He's learning that becoming whole is a practice, not a destination.

Index

C

M